Kelley has created an introspective account of how she found purpose and wellness while navigating physical challenges and the expectations of our modern lives. *The Energy Account Principle* is a poignant testament to remind ourselves of life's delicate balance and spending our energy wisely. Leaning on her faith, Kelley walks the reader through an assessment of her life's learnings, and by sharing her journey she has developed a roadmap to help others navigate trying times. *The Energy Account Principle* is honest and direct and challenges the reader to understand their true calling in life.

KEVIN K., *former colleague*

The stories and wisdom of *The Energy Account Principle* and the thoughtful questions and reflections that follow each chapter will help empower readers to pause and bring awareness to otherwise unconscious daily decisions that can build up and impact our emotional, physical, and spiritual selves. This book will feel especially relatable to the high-achieving, hard-working personalities who may have found material success through grit and resilience, yet feel burned out or unfulfilled. These reflections remind us—especially us high achieving, Type A, drivers—to accept our humanness, lean into God, and prioritize our energy for everyone's highest good.

STACEY K., *multitasking mom / wife / management executive / recovering perfectionist*

The Energy Account Principle is filled with many helpful tips backed by Kelley's real-life experience. It will make you feel less alone in a hectic world and help provide you with tools to gain control of your life. This book is relevant to all who need to find faith while calming their chaos.

BREANNE Z., *President of Community Love*

THE

Energy Account

PRINCIPLE

THE
Energy Account
✝
PRINCIPLE

Balancing Life's Challenging Choices and
Prioritizing Personal Peace in Christ

KELLEY WOTHERSPOON

credo
house publishers

Published in the United States of America by Credo House Publishers,
a division of Credo Communications LLC, Grand Rapids, Michigan
credohousepublishers.com

ISBN: 978-1-62586-185-6

Cover and interior design by Sharon VanLoozenoord
Editing by Cherry Lyn Hoffner

Printed in the United States of America
First edition

To my forever love, Brent,
and my three beautiful tornadoes:
Katey, Dex, and Gwyn.
I love you all "to the highest number."

And to Dr. Amico.
Thank you for your dedication,
commitment, and unmatched persistence
as you walked my journey beside me.
May you rest in peace.

Contents

Foreword

Imagine being an ambitious, high-performing executive in your 30s. You are thriving in your sales career and climbing the Fortune 500 corporate ladder, all while making time to serve your church community and volunteer with an organization that sets your heart on fire. At home, you prioritize and nurture relationships with your friends and family, including your supportive, loving spouse and three hilarious, rambunctious children. You're building the life you've dreamed about.

Now imagine that a medical mystery brings "life as you know it" to a screeching halt. Suddenly, you struggle to perform daily tasks. In conversation, you confuse words—and even people's names. You begin having "episodes" that include tremors, paralysis, and headaches. You lose your coveted job at the Big Company— the job that your family depends upon for financial stability.

Your debilitating symptoms continue for more than a year while you visit countless doctors to get poked, prodded, imaged, and examined. Finally, you learn that the cause of these symptoms is postpartum brain trauma—and it's gone on so long that it may not be reversible.

This is my friend Kelley's story.

Kelley and I have been best friends since sixth grade, back when Coach made us run laps during volleyball practice because we "talked too much." Our marathon conversations continue to this day—mostly over the phone now, thanks to the thousand miles that separate us. We nicknamed each other "our person," inspired by one of our favorite TV shows, *Grey's Anatomy*. Like in the show, Kelley is the Meredith to my Christina—my chosen sister and confidant. I've had a front-row seat as her story has unfolded in real time, and I've admired her grit and resilience as she's moved from merely surviving with limitations to thriving in her "new normal."

Through this book, Kelley invites us to walk alongside her on her path to physical, emotional, and spiritual recovery. Her story embodies Romans 5:3–5, which says that "suffering produces endurance, and endurance produces character, and character produces hope" [ESV].

In her suffering, Kelley has discovered hard-learned lessons about the role that energy plays in our lives—regardless of our medical condition. She borrows from economics to create *The Energy Account Principle*, a logical approach to personal energy management. She breaks down daily choices, labeling them as deposits and withdraws, to help us see how we might be able to balance our own accounts and experience peace. Her questions at the end of each chapter help us reflect on how we can put the Principle into action.

If Kelley can create a new methodology and write a book—all while managing daily limitations that resulted from brain trauma—how might her words and ideas encourage us to embrace the unexpected and step into our own families, communities, and vocations with new energy and confidence?

BETSY DEMIK

Introduction:
Let My Story Help Change Yours

Do you ever feel as though you've lost yourself in your agenda, in your ambition, in your attempts at achieving self-worth? Do you pack your schedule so full that even the slightest misstep can cause the entire day to come crashing down in a giant, fiery heap of chaos? Are you physically exhausted, mentally stretched, emotionally depleted, spiritually spent? I lived in this unhealthy state for many years and, honestly, I still fight the urge to go back despite my mountain of lessons learned. It's a tough habit to break. I've been down to the bottom of the crisis canyon and now I'm slowly climbing back out through the grace and stillness of Christ. I'm dedicated to telling my story because I hope it can help in the positive guidance of yours.

We are automatically programmed by our culture and our human nature to feel a need to establish a competitive edge and move at an unreasonable pace. We find it temporarily fulfilling, invigorating, and quite frankly necessary to be the first to reach the top, to list our day's activities as if we have somehow won the award for "Most Accomplished" based solely on our endless to-do list and the fact that we didn't spare a single moment in a 24-hour period to catch our breath. That's success, right? That's the benchmark, the goal, the disturbing reality for most of us. We fight for air as we sprint through every minute of every day with something to constantly prove. How are you? I'd dare venture to say your knee jerk response is "busy." Am I wrong?

Allow me to paint you a raw mental picture of what used to be the typical flow of my life:

Laundry, dishes, juggle kids, clean the house, feed the dogs, finish my work report, finish my daughter's school report, check in with my mom, chauffeur a kid to soccer practice, race home, pack, power nap, a ten-minute shower, a two-hour drive to the airport, a three-hour flight, check in with my husband, the baby has a fever, call the pediatrician, stuff down the feelings of helplessness and guilt, sales presentation, customer dinner, smile and look like I'm not completely exhausted, inhale a glass of wine, exhale the day's chaos, crash on the pillow. Wake up, work out, check emails, conference call, back to the airport, another three-hour flight, another two-hour drive, grab groceries, stumble through the door, cook, give baths, more dishes, more laundry, kiss husband in passing, another glass of wine, sleeping pills, bed . . . nope, the baby's crying, close my eyes, now the baby's screaming, I'm up, rock her until she's almost out, our son yells out from a night terror, our oldest daughter is stirring from the commotion, my husband is up, everyone is up, everyone is crying, more chaos, one kid is asleep, two are asleep, the third one . . . finally. It's 4 a.m., I can still get an hour and a half, focus on relaxing, tick, tock, tick, alarm buzzing, wash . . . rinse . . . repeat.

This nonstop fire drill was my autopilot existence for more years than I'd like to admit to and the eventual start of my scary tipping point. There is so much more to life than this. Please, if you get nothing else out of this book, understand that you are not designed to be a machine. You were not created to push through each revolution around the sun like you're somehow responsible to capture every millisecond and maximize it to the fullest of efficiency. Our exteriors are soft for a reason. We feel, we have limits, and we are not immune to breaking. Learn from me. Learn from my mistakes, my regrets, and my newfound hope.

I was there and I'm still in the midst of my rocky journey, but I've found continued freedom in learning to be still in the Lord. This doesn't mean inactivity; it means purposeful activity. It means activity that has a single focus—to glorify God alone with our every thought and action. I've taken all that I've learned as I make my way down this long road to physical, emotional, and spiritual recovery and developed a priority project of sorts. I'm calling it *The Energy Account Principle*. This is my belief system centered around how to manage this life in a way that brings our focus away from ourselves and back to God. It's my hope that each chapter will lead you closer to finding a balance to your existence, a purpose to your pace, and a peace for your weary soul.

Many are the plans in the mind of a man,
but it is the purpose of the Lord that will stand.
~PROVERBS 19:21~

Chapter 1

Dear 23-Year-Old Me

Dear 23-Year-Old Me,

I am writing to you from a hospital bed right now fifteen years in the future. This isn't an easy time for self-reflection, but it's an important one. In the stillness of my sterile room, I'm hooked up to an IV that is providing some much needed medicinal relief while I try not to lose my mind over the incessant beeping of a monitor that's alerting no one in particular to something clearly non-life-threatening.

Your wonderful husband, the one who married you prior to your illness but who continues to fall in love with you despite your altered state, is trying his best to sleep through the relentless noise of the annoying device and the scratching of my pen on this paper. He will be the person you unfairly channel your anger at from time to time, but he is strong, steady, and his arms can hold so much more than you ever knew. You are incredibly blessed simply for having him by your side and you will appreciate him for so many reasons.

You don't know this yet, but you will encounter other relationships prior to this one that will come with a great deal of sabotage and heartache. You'll make it through, though, because of justifications both healthy and unhealthy. By the grace of God, healthy coping styles will slowly overtake the unhealthy ones and, 10 years from now, your fiercely devoted husband will come into your life in the form of a crazy whirlwind romance anchored in divine intervention, the details of which embody a fascinating tale of their own. You will blindly cross paths for decades, but with God's perfect appointment, you will discover him (online of all places!) when you've finally experienced enough heartbreak and loss to appreciate him for all that he is and you've grown mature enough in your faith that you're progressively more open to his kind words of caution.

He will become one of the major voices of reason that points you in the right direction. This amazing man, who is snoring on a hospital pullout couch that is clearly wrecking his back with every twist and turn, will serve as a mirror image of the Lord's unbridled, steadfast, and selfless love. This walking, breathing beacon of hope is yours until death, and you will hold on to him with all that you have. You will thank your heavenly Father every day for him because this relationship has brought so much joy, comfort, and compassion into your life and the lives of your children that you won't be able to fathom going through this current trial alone.

So, let's reflect on where you are in your youth and how rearview vision will create so much perspective. We have to "live and learn," right? No one is born with an instruction manual. We have our faith, our personalities, and our paths to choose. Walk with me and we'll see the fire, the blindsiding pitfalls that drag you down from time to time, and the blessings masked in what, at first glance, seem like tragedies.

You will eventually end up in this hospital room replaying all of the twists and turns you've made over the past decade and a half. There is a crushing reality of chronic illness that has become a part of you, a permanent piece of who you are. It will forever be connected to your identity and you will learn to embrace it. In fact, you will be thankful for it because I genuinely believe it saved your life.

As I glance backward in time, I so admire your spunk, your drive, your hunger to achieve great things. These are all fantastic qualities and they are so deeply seated in you that fighting against them will only be in vain. I encourage you to foster them, grow them, sharpen them to the finest points. But I also implore you to rein them in and use them wisely. We are strong-willed, you and me. We border on obsessive compulsion and we are perfectionists in every sense of the word. We struggle with pride and believe our thoughts are higher, smarter, and will gain more traction. Sometimes they do. Sometimes we'll fail miserably, and we will take this failure to a dark and lonely place.

And I know failure is your most hated "f" word. It cuts you to the core. Looking back, I'd urge you to try an ounce of humility when you find yourself crashing into the unforgiving pavement of things gone awry. Learn from those who have gone before you and who have so much they are willing to offer by way of guidance and mentorship. Don't view them as competition, view them as allies and become a sponge. Failure at this stage, whether in your career or your life, is only an opportunity to strengthen your skills, sharpen your teeth, and build your tolerance and grit. You have nothing to lose and everything to gain.

This is ironically also the tricky side of youth. You have all the energy and none of the experience, but that's okay. It's more than okay; it's life and it's adventurous at this stage in the game. At this point, your responsibilities are few and your possibilities are endless. It's all in the balance, darling. There's a changed nature that will blossom with time. Make this personal transformation of character your heart's mission.

Upon reflection of it all, I still beg you to dream, to soar, spread your wings, and reach for the highest places. Try everything and challenge your fear of the unknown. Just keep Christ as your anchor through it all and know that there will come a time where tighter limits will have to find their place in your world, and those limits will become your lifeline. Your toughest battle will emerge when you'll eventually need to learn how to incorporate these constraints as your priorities shift.

Understand that there are seasons in life and healthy boundaries grow as we evolve ourselves in our various roles as a whole person: child of God, individual, wife, mother, professional, daughter, sister, friend. This is the concept you will struggle with the most. You'll fight the notion of parameters so intensely that it will consume every ounce of energy in you, but God's love for you will ultimately prevail. Don't worry. The next chapter of your life will be challenging, but it will stretch you to become who you were always meant to be.

In all of this personal introspection and growth, I can't stress enough that you should spend the maximum amount of your precious energy on learning to be still. This is the single most important piece of advice I can give you as it would have protected you from years of heartburn and pointless stress. That's neither here nor there now, and hindsight can't save us from our previous sins, but you will persevere and a stillness in your faith will become your most cherished possession.

Every runner requires rest. You don't see the truth in this now, but you will. You will push yourself too far as you climb that gold-plated corporate ladder. Each achievement will pale in comparison to the next and you will start to crave the addicting high of what the world deems success to be. If I could speak to you in this part of your life, I would shout so loudly imploring you to see the red flags popping up everywhere, pleading with you to notice the blazing inferno of arrows pointing to the changes in your physical health and the obsession setting in mentally. I'd beg you to pay attention to the things you are starting to sacrifice and the priorities you have so far out of order. This will be the beginning of your vicious downward spiral and you will be so blinded by financial gain, corporate titles, and bolstering accolades that it will take an act of God (literally) to bring you back down to a healthy pace.

You won't be able to change the past and this will drive your Type A personality to the edge of insanity, but you will be better for it in the end. You will take each of these experiences and stack them up to allow you to reach your apex of change. Not only will you survive this, you will actually thrive because of it.

Hang in there, 23-year-old me. You have so much to give, you just won't know how until life brings you to your knees. Only then will you stand up on more solid ground, dust yourself off, accept what is healthy and begin walking forward in the aura of newfound faith. The best is yet to come, but it's not the picture you had originally painted. It's more of a Picasso, but that only adds to its interesting characteristics. You will no longer have to micromanage every situation and fear the uncertainties. You will have God by your side and the wind of your support system at your back. You will find a greatness beyond yourself and you'll be able to enjoy it so much more because of how far you've come!

I'm better for having been you!
38-Year-Old Me

Insights

What are some of the reflections you can make about unhealthy mindsets, attitudes, and habits that you adopted in your past?

_____

_____

_____

How have you overcome some of these? Which ones are you still holding on to?

_____

_____

_____

Actions

Write a letter to your past self, praising the healthy aspects and forgiving the not-so-healthy. You'd be surprised how therapeutic this is and the weight it will lift off your spirit!

_____

_____

_____

_____

_____

If you have given your life over to Christ by accepting him as your Savior, pray that he will help you let go of past baggage and allow you to move forward with a newfound sense of grace and confidence. Forgiveness happens daily. We need only to accept him once but that doesn't mean his grace and mercy fall in the "one and done" category. He's with us for the entire ride.

_____

_____

_____

_____

If you have not committed your life to Christ, consider the gospel. The Bible recounts a lost world in need of the kind of healing that only God can provide. He sent his Son, Jesus, to pay for our sins on the cross so that we can be equipped with the guidance of the Holy Spirit in this life and ultimately spend eternity with him in the next. Heaven is a Christian's destination, but saving faith is so much more than that. We get to embrace an existence on earth that is infused with a hope and purpose beyond our own. We're part of something so much bigger. Your presence in Christ will open your eyes to a meaning that is rooted in service and sacrifice, not self and security. All he asks of you is to call upon his name in prayer longing to become a child of his and for the God of this universe to sit on the throne of your heart.

_____

_____

_____

_____

Chapter 2

The Energy Account Principle:
My Philosophy on Conquering the Chaos

ENERGY ACCOUNT	
DEPOSIT	**WITHDRAWAL**
Beginning to Master the Art of Balance	*Continuing to Barrel toward Energy Bankruptcy*

As someone who suffers from chronic illness, I can relate to others in similar situations. Plenty of physicians and specialists have formed notions, philosophies, and suggestions around the best ways to monitor energy output and how to utilize what little vigor we do have in the healthiest and most efficient ways possible. As we attempt to face our daily lives feeling drained and run down a strong majority of the time, we have to take care how much effort we exert and when we exert it. Our consistent and persistent physical, mental, and emotional depletions including pain, fatigue, and an occasional overall inability to function set us apart from someone who does not live with these types of ailments.

While I think these guardrails and parameters are so helpful and needed in the chronic condition circle, dare I go so far as to say that maybe . . . just maybe . . . we are all facing a common chronic condition in our modern world? I've let you peer through the window of my soul as you've witnessed bits and pieces of my current medical drama and my longing to give my 23-year-old self advice that may have changed the future course of my health. Can you relate to the daily chaos of moving at an ungodly pace? Do you feel the pressures of social media perfection, friends in higher places, houses outside of your own that are pristine enough to be featured on the cover of *Better Homes and Gardens*? Are you with me?

I strongly believe that there's an epidemic plaguing our modern society. It's a condition in which enough is never enough, more is king, and stillness is the enemy. If you're not "busy," you're viewed as "lazy" and, God forbid, we don't measure up to the expectations of everyone around us! We have to perform, perfect, please, and pursue. The important skill of learning how to rest is viewed as only for the people who are left in the dust, as most of us set ourselves to a mode labeled "hyper speed" and trample over them in a race to some elusive finish line—only to find that the finish line is a lie. It's merely another notch in our belts, a benchmark to push us to the next coveted goal.

Sure, this may pad our bank accounts for a while and buy our next fancy toy, but what is it doing to our health? According to an article in *USA Today*,[1] the top 10 illnesses plaguing the people in our country from birth to age 64 include:

1. Hypertension – National Health Impact 12.5%
2. Major Depression – National Health Impact 9%
3. High Cholesterol – National Health Impact 8.6%
4. Coronary Artery Disease – National Health Impact 7%
5. Type 2 Diabetes – National Health Impact 5.5%
6. Substance Use Disorder – National Health Impact 3.4%
7. Alcohol Use Disorder – National Health Impact 3.3%
8. COPD – National Health Impact 3.3%
9. Psychotic Disorder – National Health Impact 2.9%
10. Crohn's Disease/Ulcerative Colitis – National Health Impact 2.7%

The grim reality is that each condition on this list can be in some way caused or worsened by stress. When I started experi-

---

1 Kate Morgan for Blue Cross Blue Shield Association, "These are the Top 10 Health Conditions Affecting Americans," USA Today, October 24, 2018, https://www.usatoday.com/story/sponsor-story/blue-cross-blue-shield-association/2018/10/24/these-top-10-health-conditions-affecting-americans/1674894002/.

encing symptoms of my chronic illnesses, my gut response was to figure out how to manage my body around my career. This was so backward that I'm almost embarrassed to admit it. But in the moment, I had an incredible position at an extraordinary company with a bright future to move up and make the kind of money that would set my family up for years to come. The problem was that the harder I tried to prioritize my success over my health, the worse I suffered in both categories. I was in a sinking ship that was filling with water at an increased speed while I stood there trying to bail myself out with nothing but a tiny ladle. A change was inevitable. Eventually, I had to succumb to a disability arrangement because my physical and mental capabilities were declining and I needed to stop the waves before my boat completely sank.

At this point, I began to take a long hard look at my life. What had I sacrificed and how much was it worth in relation to the state I was in now? Is ambition bad? Not at all! Is it wrong to love your career and strive to perform well at your job? Certainly not! Should we never dream or push ourselves to achieve our goals and aspirations? I say, dream and push *to a healthy limit*. This shapes us as people and satisfies our souls, but we have to better understand that these same qualities can become soul-crushing if we are not on our guard.

This is where my principle comes in—it's called The Energy Account Principle and I wholeheartedly believe it can apply to anyone reading this. Young, old, healthy, ill, confident, confused, we can all benefit from a balanced account in life. Let me explain.

I'm willing to bet that you have experience with a financial account in some way. I assume that you have been tasked with the actions of spending and saving money around various wants and needs. There are a number of scenarios that accompany your funds. I'm going to categorize these into five general groups:

1. Surplus due to funds worked for and saved over time.
2. Surplus due to funds given to us with no repayment requirements (i.e., an inheritance or a donation from a family member or charitable organization).
3. Break-even.

4. Debt due to funds borrowed as a result of circumstances outside of our control (i.e., loss of a job) or in preparation for future gain (i.e., college tuition, purchasing a home within our limits of financial margin).
5. Debt due to funds borrowed as a result of prioritizing wants over needs (i.e., purchasing a home or vehicle that exceeds the limits of our financial margin).

If you've had any exposure to Economics 101, you know that we are ideally supposed to live in the security of group #1. Group #2 is a blessing but not a guarantee or permanent solution to any sustainable financial planning. Group #3 is toeing a very dangerous line. Group #4 is less than ideal but it often revolves around a season in our lives as opposed to a long term way of living. Group #5 is where I believe quite a few of us tend to live in our country today. Our homes are not big enough, our cars are not nice enough, our clothes are not stylish enough, our accessories are not shiny enough, and our (fill in the blank here) are not new enough.

We are constantly living with something to prove and dying with a whole lot of "stuff" that we can't take with us in the end. Meanwhile, the space between our birth and death dates is consumed with this ever-expanding stressor called interest. It is rarely forgiven and sometimes mounts so high that it's nearly impossible to pay back. We get to a point where we feel buried, helpless, and sometimes we get so far into debt that we realistically can't recover barring a miracle.

As I've navigated the choppy waters of the various aspects of my overall health, I've seen an uncanny comparison to the same patterns that apply to financial health. As such, I've developed the Energy Account Principle defined as follows:

The Energy Account Principle is grounded in biblical truths and based on the belief that we all have a reserve of energy (our energy accounts) requiring a positive balance to preserve physical, mental, emotional, and spiritual well-being. While all theories have exceptions and outliers, the choices we make about our attitudes, actions, relationships, thoughts, and desires will either contribute to or withdraw from our energy accounts. If our energy accounts remain positive, we can typically sustain a situation of overall health. If we allow our accounts to encounter a negative balance, however, we will most likely begin to draw against an energy loan of sorts and this borrowed energy will need to be paid back with interest. Such interest involves the sacrifice of our overall well-being and can lead to energy bankruptcy if steps aren't taken to restore our energy account to a positive state.

Based on The Energy Account Principle, the five categories that break down positions relating to health as opposed to finance can be reflected in the following way:

1. Surplus due to energy worked for and saved over time—this would essentially encompass how we manage our stress and our schedules to achieve a healthy balance of prioritized faith, personal achievement, and recreational activity.
2. Surplus due to energy given to us with no repayment required—this would include situations where friends and family members help us out with no strings attached (i.e., grandparents who are willing to watch the kids so you can take time for a date night, a friend who voluntarily offers her organizational skills to help get your house in order, people who bring periodic meals after you've had surgery).
3. Break-even—the energy you're expending is equal to the rest you are achieving, and one tiny straw could cause this camel to have a mental and physical meltdown.
4. Debt due to the energy borrowed as a result of circumstances outside of our control or with the intention of sacrifice now for future gain. Divorce, the death of a loved one, a cancer diagnosis—these are a few examples that would fall into this category. Sometimes life changes direction without our consent and we will have to struggle through for a period of time no matter how much energy we try to conserve. Following this same principle, but under very different circumstances, sometimes we are willing to push ourselves beyond our immediate limits (i.e., planning for a wedding, pulling all-nighters to pass a final) because we know that, in time, we will be better positioned to bring our lives back into balance. We can live in this space for a season but

eventually, our energy savings will be depleted, and we need to plan to regain our positive balance.

5. Debt due to energy borrowed as a result of prioritizing wants over needs. This is the land of the not-so-free and the home of the enslaved. This, my friends, is the rat race we run on the hamster wheel of success, esteem, and the monetary mirage. We think that if we just push a little harder, work a little longer, and dig a little deeper, we will finally reach the top of the elusive mountain of contentment. But we never get there, and we do it all at the expense of sleep, meaningful relationships, precious time, our connection with our Savior, and eventually our health. *This* is the place I fear most of us live and the very devastating quicksand I'm urging each of us to start pulling ourselves out of before we sink so far into energy debt that we become suffocated by the heaviness of it all. We can only pay on the interest at this point and this repayment is solely achieved through the sacrifice of our quality of life. Nothing is worth this. Nothing.

So, here's the good news. We can all make changes in our energy accounts at any point in our lives. Just like any competent financial planner would tell you regarding your money, take an honest look at where you are *now* and make a plan for where you want to be. Once you have your long-term goal in mind, start *today*. Waiting until it's convenient will only make you less likely to start at all.

And for the record, this will never be convenient. It takes hard work, a strong measure of discipline, a commitment to digging our heels into the solid ground of biblical truths, and an uncanny ability to know when to say "no." It really is no different from managing your finances, and I strongly believe that this type of management will have a far greater impact on how you live out this one chance at life.

So, what does this look like? Here's a practical example:

Let's say you want to work no more than 40 hours a week, you desire to start attending church consistently, you want to be freed up to coach your son's baseball team, you've got to start eating a healthier diet, and you know you need to begin averaging eight hours of sleep each night. If your job requires a one-hour commute, you're working minimally nine hours a day on top of that commute, you're grabbing whatever fast food is the quickest option so that you can get back to your desk and work through your lunch, you're constantly "on call" by checking emails and putting out every fire that occurs after your normal workday ends, and Sunday has become your day of catching up instead of your day of rest and worship, then your energy account is being drained and something has to drastically change if you are going to reach your goal of positive energy well-being.

We only have 24 hours in a day. It's our commitment to ourselves and to our Creator to use our time wisely. Let's take the above scenario and find some realistic solutions to achieve our maximum energy account value. A one-hour commute each way equates to 10 hours a week. Assuming between vacation time and holidays you work 49 weeks out of a given year, this is 490 hours of your life or a little over 20 *days*. What can you do about this? Can you move closer to your place of employment? Can you request to work from home a few days a week? Can you find another employer with a similar upside but that is in better proximity to your home? You have choices, they might just not be easy ones.

The same goes for a demanding position that is requiring you to commit far beyond your desired 40-hour workweek. Can you work smarter? Are there things you can delegate? Can you opt for another position that gives you the same degree of satisfaction but demands less of your free time? "But," you argue, "the money might be less, and it could be a step backward in my career!" That's okay, it's worth every penny in relation to the quality of life you will gain.

Insights

In what ways are you currently depleting your energy account?
Have you had any physical, emotional, or spiritual issues that might possibly serve as warning signs that it's time to shift gears a bit?

_____

_____

_____

_____

What are some areas in your life that you feel are marked with good balance? Why?

_____

_____

_____

_____

Actions

Make a list of three small actions you can set into motion right now to take steps toward undoing unhealthy habits that are draining you and taking your focus away from what God's plan is for your life.

_____

_____

_____

_____

Create a visual roadmap of where you are now in relation to where your physical, emotional, and spiritual priorities need to be. Start with a written list of future positive goals. Work through possible solutions to any current circumstances that are holding you back. Use this clarity to construct benchmarks along a timeline to maintain a solid plan. And allow some flexibility as God may have something even better in store as you begin to walk a more Christ-centered path!

_____

_____

_____

_____

_____

_____

Chapter 3

My Story . . . So Far

ENERGY ACCOUNT	
DEPOSIT	**WITHDRAWAL**
Learning to Let Go	*Holding on to Unhealthy*

I was there, my friend. I lived it. I once worked for a company that was so demanding of my time and energy that even though I had a delayed flight and got home from a customer meeting at midnight, I was still expected to be in the office by 8 a.m. the next morning (a reprieve from the 7:30 a.m. start time I was typically held to). Forget any sort of comp time for the eighteen-plus hours I had just put in the day before, the concepts of "mercy" or "grace" didn't exist in their inflexible vocabulary. Employees were nothing more than an impersonal cog in their self-serving wheel. This was further solidified as someone from the company called me an hour after a close family member passed away (this colleague was well aware of my loss) for help with a technical question because it was easier to "just take a few minutes of my time" as opposed to respecting my need for privacy to grieve. The deal-breaker for me came when leadership within the company did something inconceivable involving denying me the time and space I needed to care for one of my kids. I wish I was joking. Looking back, I'm disappointed in myself that it took something this dehumanizing to finally push me to move on. Toxic environments like this drag us into an unhealthy cycle that is tough to break.

I eventually found a home in another company that treated me like a respected human being with valid feelings and instituted realistic limits. Unfortunately, I believe that I had been so mentally beaten into working like a machine that the cycle was near impossible to reverse. Cue the birth of my third child—a bouncing baby girl that triggered all the happy feels but also a rare migraine condition called Hemiplegic Migraines (HM). Ten days postpartum, my physical decline wasn't quite finished, and I ended up hospitalized for three days with postpartum pre-eclampsia (pre-e). This perfect storm of HM and pre-e sent my brain into overdrive and I developed an even more rare condition called PPRCVS (Postpartum Reversible Cerebral Vasoconstriction Syndrome).

This was only the beginning of a grueling journey that would take 19 months of tests, invasive procedures, and countless specialists scratching their heads. I had several scary symptoms including cognitive impairment, daily mild left-side paralysis, fatigue, language and visual deficits, and ataxia (impaired coordination and balance) before we landed on a diagnosis. By the time I had a viable explanation, my brain had been deprived of proper blood flow for far too long and it was possible that I had developed mild brain damage, which may or may not be reversible. I started experiencing episodic dystonic spasms in my neck which is a potentially lifelong, stress-induced condition that causes my neck muscles to tense up and jerk backward. During these episodes, I also lose my ability to speak. It can be incredibly painful as the muscles in my neck tighten and it is *never* worth the stressful situation that I allowed my mind and body to be subjected to.

These circumstances have caused our entire family to struggle more deeply than we ever thought possible. As I mentioned before, I was placed on disability cutting my bread-winning income in half. My husband, Brent, picked up more shifts to try to fill in some of the financial gaps which created an additional level of taxing complexity. I made several trips to the ER each time I'd have an episode, and we endured more testing, more specialists, and more questions. Our kids were clearly scared to death and acting out in their own ways as they made attempts to cope with so many changes all at once. Life got scary, but these rock-bottom moments always seem to force our eyes up.

Something amazing began to happen in the midst of our despair. Our faith in God grew immensely, and boy, did he come through in all of his promises to provide. When we were short on money because Brent had to call off to take care of me, we'd get a check in the mail for some random refund we hadn't even realized we had coming. When I was too fatigued to make my family dinner, our friends would show up with a meal. When I couldn't function because my vertigo literally took me to my knees, our family would step in to wrangle our little crazies and fill in the gaps wherever they could. We have been blessed in unimaginable ways outside of our circumstances, and we've had the incredible opportunity to learn firsthand that our Lord has an impeccable track record for imparting his grace on his children beyond our immediate understanding of his perfect timing.

So, does this mean our path is now easy-peasy and we're walking on sunshine? Not even close. Our days are still hard, some much harder than others. We attended therapy sessions to help us adjust. I also joined a grief group to help deal with the relinquishing of my profession in the way I had previously known it and the new limitations that were placed on how I should manage my daily life. When a doctor tells you point-blank that you'll never quite be one hundred percent of your former self again and that it is not reasonable to go back to the pace of the career you've spent 15 years building, it's a giant punch to your gut and a massive blow to your ego. But it's also a much-needed wakeup call.

You see, it was time to face a harsh but critical reality. My energy account had accumulated so much debt that I had hit physical bankruptcy. It was necessary to cut my losses, reevaluate my priorities, and start to build my account back up to a healthy point. I am still struggling. There are so many instances when I catch myself starting to succumb to my old ways and I begin to push beyond what's in my energy account. I start to borrow beyond my means and have to force myself to stick to my plan for peace.

This really is no different from what it takes to dig out of a financial loss. It calls for practice, discipline, and accountability. When I slide back into my old energy-spending habits from time to time, and there's a spiritual siren that the Holy Spirit sounds to alert me when I'm stepping too close to the edge, I remind myself of all the reasons why I don't ever want to go back to that devastation. If my efforts fail, God will block my path, Brent won't hesitate to call me out in order to reel me back into balance, and my friends and family will perform an honest check-in to gauge how well I'm really doing. I'm so thankful for all of these checks and balances.

I know I don't have this rhythm down perfectly yet, but I'm closer than I've ever been. If the gut punch of some sort of physical, mental, or spiritual decline has already brought you to your bankruptcy point in your energy account, you are not alone. Hope is on the horizon, and you too can start to rebuild. If you have not reached that point but you know you're on a slippery slope, turn around *now*. You'll look back at this decision with all the happiness and joy it will bring and what sacrifices you think you're making will pale in comparison to a life overflowing with better health, peace, and purpose.

Insights

What situations are you currently tolerating simply because you don't want to face a change? What impact is this having on your energy account?

_____

_____

_____

Can you recall a time when you witnessed God come through on his promises for your life at a point when you felt all hope might be in vain?

_____

_____

_____

Actions

Dedicate some time to pray specifically asking God to reveal areas of your life where you need to relinquish control and release over to the Lord's care.

_____

_____

_____

Identify one healthy habit that you can institute right now *to replace something unhealthy in your life.*

_____

_____

_____

Chapter 4

Strength in the Stillness

ENERGY ACCOUNT	
DEPOSIT	**WITHDRAWAL**
Finding a Peace to Your Pace	*Moving at the Speed of "Me"*

Impatience is a form of unbelief. It's what we begin to feel when we start to doubt the wisdom of God's timing of the goodness of his guidance. It springs up in our hearts when the road to success gets muddy, or strewn with boulders, or blocked by some fallen tree. The battle with impatience can be a little skirmish over a long wait in a checkout lane. Or, it can be a major combat over a handicap, or a disease, or circumstance that knocks out half your dreams.[1]
~JOHN PIPER~

This concept, dear friends, was and remains my greatest nemesis. Telling me to slow down is like asking a cheetah to decelerate to a casual jog. I'm wired to be wired. I run on caffeine and an internal drive that only knows one speed—full throttle. My motivational lead foot keeps my brain moving a million miles an hour, and I pile so many things into my daily checklist that it would

---

1   John Piper, "Battling the Unbelief of Impatience," November 27, 1988, https://www.desiringgod.org/messages/battling-the-unbelief-of-impatience.

take a week to cross everything off. Not only is this unrealistic, but it's also unhealthy, it sets me up for failure, and it's a giant energy account withdrawal.

Does this sound a bit familiar with regard to the way you jam-pack your own schedule? "But there are so many things I have to get done," you may argue. Agreed. But there are also so many things you *won't* get done if you create an expectation that will only lead to a state of exhaustion and burnout. According to an article in *Forbes* titled, "The Truth About Why You're Overcommitted,"[2] our culture, combined with our internal need to feel accomplished and important, has conditioned us to be all things to all people at all times at any expense—particularly the expense of our energy accounts. In the article, author Demir Bentley tells us the story of Sarah whom I imagine we can all relate to in some way. Sarah was essentially taking on every project thrown at her professionally resulting in next to no time for herself personally. Even though she knew she was overloaded, she was drowning in a "constant state of overcommitment." Sarah's issue was causing physical problems that included premature aging and declining health. According to Bentley,

> *Sarah is more the rule than the exception. Did you know that the United States is the only industrialized country in the world without a legal maximum amount of hours you can work per week? On average, professionals work enough hours a week to equal an entire extra workday!*
>
> *. . . The truth about overcommitment is hard to hear . . . It should be no surprise that some of the most successful people are chronically overcommitted—it's what we've been raised to do . . .*
>
> *But constantly saying yes to everything isn't pushing us forward. In fact, it's keeping you from growing, fast-tracking you to burnout and reinforcing a slew of mindset issues.*

For the record, this "Sarah" scenario doesn't just apply to the sharply-dressed executive clawing his or her way up the slippery

---

2   Demir Bentley, "The Truth About Why You're Overcommitted," *Forbes*, March 29, 2018, https://www.forbes.com/sites/forbescoachescouncil/2018/03/29/the-truth-about-why-youre-overcommitted/#3783bfd36709.

rungs of the corporate ladder in the hopes of achieving a corner office in the C-Suite. This is every stay-at-home mom or dad multitasking the heaping dishes, piles of laundry, constant diaper changes, and daunting weekly run to the grocery store (and then the second run for all the things that were forgotten!). This is every blue-collar worker straddling the line between meeting the daily quota, pleasing the overbearing boss, and trying to conserve enough energy to be a spouse, parent, or social human being by the time he or she walks through the door of their home. This is all of us and we need to break this cycle—now!

I was once at a customer meeting during which two of the individuals in attendance started comparing how few hours of sleep they could get away with regularly and still function. "I start work around 7 a.m., take a little break once I get home from the office, and start up again once my wife and kids are in bed around nine or ten," one of them bragged. "Then I'll take a two- or three-hour power nap and get right back at it until it's time to arrive back at the office again." I sat quietly in my cushy chair, feeling like a failure for trying to achieve six to eight hours a night. I started thinking to myself, *How could I be so lazy as to "waste" this precious work time with sleeping? How will I ever be able to keep up in the big leagues if I've got the work habits of a minor league player?*

This is the recipe for a serious health disaster, an inevitable mental meltdown, or a speed pass to an early grave at some point when our bodies no longer care about what our egos are striving to accomplish. The sooner we realize that pushing too hard to outwork, outshine, outperform, and outlast the competition is just plain stupid, the sooner we can find a much-needed release and the permission to function at a God-intended pace. This pace will become a major deposit into our energy accounts, and we will start to feel a peaceful satisfaction in the lives we're living. We'll begin to move toward our true purpose in Christ and feel that our actions truly matter because the quality far surpasses the quantity.

To fight withdrawing from our energy accounts by "moving at the speed of me," we need to find the ability to be still in the purposes of honoring God through his allowance of space to be available to the service of others. Our ultimate goal as Christians isn't merely to excel within our vocation, it's to be useful outside of it as well.

One of my favorite social experiments was performed by behavioral scientists John Darley and Daniel Batson on Princeton theology students back in the 1970s.[3] It goes a little something like this:

> *Participants were all told that they needed to walk to a nearby building to meet up with another member of the team and then give their sermon. They then, by random chance, were determined to be in one of three conditions. They either were told that they:*
>
> *A. had plenty of time and were early.*
> *B. were on-time but should head over now so as not to be late.*
> *Or*
> *C. were running late and really needed to skedaddle.*

Unbeknownst to the participants, they found a fallen stranger (who was actually part of the experiment) in an alleyway that was so narrow the students would have to literally step over him if they didn't stop to help!

Ready for the results? Here's what Darley and Batson found:

> *People who reported as religious for intrinsic reasons were no more likely than others to stop and help.*
> *The "time-constraint" variable mattered a ton.*
> *63% of participants in the "early" condition stopped to help the stranger.*
> *45% of participants in the "on-time" condition stopped to help the stranger.*
> *10% of participants in the "late" condition stopped to help the stranger.*

If we pack our lives with a schedule that revolves one hundred percent around our own goals and aspirations with no space to

3   Glenn Geher PhD, "My Favorite Psychology Study," *Psychology Today*, March 16, 2017, https://www.psychologytoday.com/us/blog/darwins-subterranean-world/201703/my-favorite-psychology-study.

catch our breath, we have zero time left to be a blessing to others. Dedicating time to simply be still not only provides rest required of our weary souls, but it also strengthens our spirits by allowing us to be open to blessing others. This will, no doubt, make a large deposit into our energy accounts *and* into the energy accounts of the people we get the opportunity to serve. Even Jesus himself carved time out of his ministry to sit in the stillness of his Father's presence to both gain a moment of meaningful rest and prepare to be a vessel for God's ultimate will. There's so much good that can happen in this space.

So, I'd like to bring this home on a practical level. Dare I suggest that we look at the objective for our days in the same way Jesus did? What if we looked at time differently? What if, instead of tackling one day as a single number, we divided it up into the hours it's composed of? And what if those hours were separated out into realistic percentages of time that would hold us accountable to both our healthy priorities and also to our additional unclaimed minutes purposed to be spent well on being accessible to others?

May I suggest the following as a loose outline of a typical weekday (this applies to the stay-at-home parent, the full-time employee, and anyone in between) and then urge you to use your weekends to worship corporately, catch up, unwind, rest, play, enjoy, and be of more service if needed:

    33% (8 hours)—work (defined by your specific situation)
    33% (8 hours)—sleep
    9% (2 hours)—family time
    9% (2 hours)—household obligations (i.e., mow the lawn, dishes, etc.)
    4% (1 hour)—margin for being available
    4% (1 hour)—physical activity
    4% (1 hour)—God time/meditation/reflection
    4% (1 hour)—me time

Please keep in mind that this concept needs to come with a measure of grace. You will need a strong commitment of fortitude, but it will also be impossible to hold to this one hundred percent of the time. Keep at it the best you can and watch your energy account start to gain *positive* interest! You will be so much better off if you make a concerted effort to try. As this becomes more of a habit and less of a chore, it will also become a desire of your heart. And the awkwardness of the structure of it all will be replaced by the God-given fulfillment that flows from your time well spent. Christlikeness and genuine kindness will become the motivations for your time management, and, because of these reasons, you will suddenly uncover so many ways to be available to others without the guilt and desire to revert to self-preservation. Let go of your white-knuckle grip and allow the Lord to carry you with his unbreakable assurances of security and grace. There is no greater freedom and fulfillment in this life!

Insights

What are the top three areas of your life in which you struggle to be still and relinquish control of your time (i.e., career, parenting, money)?

_____

_____

_____

_____

Can you think of a specific time that you missed an opportunity to help someone else because you were too busy "moving at the speed of me"? Did you regret not being available? How about a time when you were available to assist someone else? How did you feel in that situation?

_____

_____

_____

_____

_____

_____

Actions

Commit to implementing the timeline percentages outlined above with the understanding that this will take time and practice. Log your current activities to see which category each activity falls in within the 24-hour period and make small adjustments until you're closer to the end goal.

_____

_____

_____

_____

_____

_____

Focus specifically on leaving some "Good Samaritan" time in your schedule every day and pay attention to how God might choose to use those moments as a way for you to show his love to others.

_____

_____

_____

_____

Chapter 5

The Power of Acceptance

ENERGY ACCOUNT	
DEPOSIT	**WITHDRAWAL**
A Spirit of Joy in All Situations	*A Need for Constant Control*

Let your joy be in your journey, not in some distant goal.
~TIM COOK~

Hi, my name is Kelley Wotherspoon and I'm a true-blue, bonified control freak. I admit it, it's interwoven into the deepest parts of my DNA and it is incredibly difficult for me to accept anything that's outside of this control that I covet so unhealthily. But admission is the first step, right?

I know this about myself and, because I can identify it, I can start down a path of positive change. This has undoubtedly been my toughest character trait to work on, but I feel confident that as long as I'm making honest strides toward improvement, I'll be better today than yesterday and then even better tomorrow. This is all God asks of me. He has promised to take care of the rest. My only job is to trust him enough that I am able to truly let go of my past sins, believe in the power of his forgiveness, and keep moving.

The irony of working toward a spirit of joy as opposed to a spirit of control is that I have to relinquish my control as part of the methodology moving forward—something that initially feels painful and counterintuitive, but will actually bring me joy! You see, a spirit of joy is outside of anything I can manufacture within myself. It is a quality gifted by God alone, and one in which I have to ultimately rely on him to change within me. God and I, we've wrestled—man have we wrestled! He has tried in so many gentle ways to ease me into a life of joy beyond various oscillating circumstances and I have essentially told him to shove it. I know this sounds blunt but, if I'm being completely honest and transparent, I have spent the majority of my adult life convinced that I know better than the God who made me and who has a purpose for me far beyond my limited understanding of what seems to make sense in my one-track mind.

I have made so many choices based on my own ambitions, my own desires, my own foolish interpretations of what I think is best in the moment to reach some elusive goal later. Clearly, joy had no place in this process as I would constantly move through the roller coaster of ups and downs with matching emotion. Something good would take place and I'd be on cloud nine. Five minutes later, something caused the good to fall through and I'd be left wallowing in the trenches. This state of instability is not what God intends for us. Joy is an attitude that is not dependent on any external environment, and it is the very thing that keeps us moving even when life does its best to paralyze our souls.

James 1:2–3 says to "count it all joy, my brothers, when you meet trials of various kinds, for you know that the testing of your faith produces steadfastness."

Thank the Lord that he is only patient to a point. I know this statement sounds backward but the following explanation will shed some more light. You see, our Father will softly whisper and gently prod until finally he does what any good and loving parent would do—he uses discipline and redirection to move us away from the things that are perpetually hurting us.

The breakdown of my body was no accident. It was not random. The timing was perfect, and it allowed the Lord to meet me at a place where my heart and mind didn't have much left in them to fight back anymore. My spirit was broken and nearing a point where I would be ready to listen, mostly because I would have nowhere else to turn and there would be no more I could do in my own strength. I was in a "time out" of sorts, but I came to know it was because my heavenly Father loved me too much to continue to let me live a life of chaos and constant self-preservation.

Now, don't misunderstand me. I wasn't some perfectly obedient child who removed my nose from the corner and wholly accepted this new direction for my life. I didn't peacefully leave my old ways behind initially. I went kicking and screaming and throwing every tantrum under the sun. I've had a harder head and heart throughout this process than I'd like to admit, but God's unfailing grace covered that, too. He created my personality and he also knew how to mold it into something beautiful.

But because of that, he foreknew that this journey wouldn't be a smooth one. I'm so thankful that the Lord is in this with me for the long haul and that he doesn't give up on his children when we push him away with both arms. Instead, he loves us unconditionally and gently pulls us back in despite the undeserving prodigal sons and daughters that we are.

Now, being strong-willed and persistent don't have to be negative qualities. They have actually served me quite well in life and I've survived things I'm not sure I would have had I not possessed this internal grit. But there are two sides to every character trait, and we have to be willing to be sculpted to utilize these traits for the precise reasons they've been given to us.

We are each a product of God's intricate design, not some random accident derived from happenstance. Our talents, abilities, and personalities are *exactly* what they are supposed to be to position us for our greater purpose in this life. When we learn how to relinquish control of who we are now to understand who we are meant to be in Christ, and when we can derive a sense of peace from a situation despite the absence of any reason for happiness, it is *then* that we know we've come to accept true joy.

You see, joy and happiness are not synonymous. Happiness is fleeting and circumstantial; joy is an attitude that is ingrained within us. As I write this, we are in the midst of the coronavirus pandemic, and I think these types of uncontrolled catastrophes illuminate who among us responds with an internal sense of unfaltering joy in troubled times or an internal sense of panic out of a desire for control that doesn't exist. Some things just *are*, and I believe God allows both abundance and tragedy to challenge our hearts at the cellular level.

The Book of Job is a perfect account of a man who gave his entire heart to God and yet the Lord permitted Satan to inject an incredible amount of pain into his life. Job cried out, he despised his situation, and he grieved in the deepest parts of his soul. He had questions for God, but he never questioned the intentions or love of God. His entire life was in shambles, but his joy remained steadfast in the Lord.

Another example is the heartbreaking story of Horatio Spafford. Spafford, a successful attorney and the recipient of many blessings during his life, suddenly lost his four-year-old son, and then the Great Chicago Fire of 1871 put him in financial ruin. The economic downturn in 1873 drove him down even further. Spafford had planned to travel to Europe with his family but decided last minute to send them on ahead while he stayed back to deal with some additional business-related issues. He planned to meet them once his matters were ironed out.

The ship carrying Spafford's family across the Atlantic Ocean collided with another vessel and quickly sank. He was devastated to learn that all four of his daughters had perished in the accident when he received a telegram from his wife that in its sad simplicity stated, "Saved alone . . . " As Spafford made his way across the same ocean to get to his grieving wife, he found inspiration in the very spot where the other ship had sunk. The words he penned have become a famous hymn in our churches today:

> *When peace like a river, attendeth my way,*
> *When sorrows like sea billows roll;*
> *Whatever my lot, thou hast taught me to say,*
> *It is well, it is well with my soul.*

> *Though Satan should buffet, though trials should come,*
> *Let this blest assurance control:*
> *That Christ has regarded my helpless estate,*
> *And has shed his own blood for my soul.*

My sin, oh, the bliss of this glorious thought!
My sin, not in part, but the whole,
Is nailed to the cross, and I bear it no more;
Praise the Lord, praise the Lord, O my soul!

It is well with my soul;
It is well, it is well with my soul.[1]

My physical condition has taken me away from the career I worked so hard to build; I get what it's like to feel as though the rug of my professional identity has been abruptly pulled out from underneath me. Our economy is currently in crisis, my 401(k) is in a present state of annihilation, and my income has been cut in half due to my disability. I can relate in some minimal way to the taste of financial ruin on the heels of longstanding profit and success. What I can't fathom is the loss of my children. Like Spafford, I have a four-year-old son. I also have two daughters that sandwich my little guy in the middle. Losing any one of my babies would be enough to wreck my world for the rest of my days. Losing all three—I'm not sure my heart could withstand that height of anguish.

I don't know your set of circumstances; you may have experienced loss far beyond my comprehension. Spafford clearly did and yet he was able to endure it with joy. This is the kind of joy, my dear friends, that we can all be graciously given through Christ, and it's the kind of joy I desire to find my soul filled with in time. It's precisely this joy that would keep our eyes fixed on Christ despite our standing with this world. It will steady us in the most abundant of times and see us through the most tragic of times.

In light of all the catastrophic loss we've spoken of, there was one individual who has encountered a more unbearable pain than any of us will ever know. Jesus himself endured the literal pits of hell so that we could be spared the unimaginable eternity we deserve as sinners. The beauty of the gospel that secured our souls was bought with a price so devastating for Jesus that

1   Horatio Gates Spafford, "It is Well with My Soul," 1873.

he cried out, "Father, if you are willing, remove this cup from me. Nevertheless, not my will, but yours, be done" (Luke 22:42). It wasn't that he didn't wish for our salvation to be achieved, he wanted this with his entire being. It was the fact that his role in saving our souls would not come easily. Jesus grieved his inevitable fate so intensely that he sweat drops of blood. I can't imagine that he felt an ounce of happiness in all of this, but his joy in his Father was unwavering, nonetheless.

Jesus is our ultimate example. Oh, how I long to know this level of completeness in joy. Someday, heaven will afford me this luxury; until then I'll aspire to get as close as I can. And it's tough, so incredibly tough, at times to find joy in horrible circumstances or seasons of our lives. The fireball of the spiritual learning curve burns like no pain we've ever felt before, but it also purifies. It refines us and we are better for it in the end. I'm so thankful that the Lord loves each of us enough to bring us through this fire with the providence of his perfect timing. I'm personally not completely out of this furnace yet, but I am gaining a deeper acceptance of its purpose in my life.

Choose joy. The relinquishing of control will be flat out frightening at first. It will feel somewhat backward in the beginning stages of this growth process, but you'll come out on the other side of it with a peace that truly passes all earthly understanding. Our God loves us too much to let us go. He's got a divine plan for each of us and he longs to use us for his greater glory. We're tools in his hands, but a lot of times we are tools that need to be sharpened before we can truly be effective. So, jump into the flames with both feet. You won't regret it; you'll rise from the ashes to a life you never knew you could have and with a sense of joy that will define the rest of your days.

It seems entirely fitting to end this chapter with a quote by Mother Teresa, a woman who embodied so much joy in the midst of so much hardship:

> *The best way to show my gratitude to God is to accept everything, even my problems, with joy!*

Insights

Do you currently feel like you find joy in the midst of life's various journeys or is the concept of joy something you view more as an end goal? Why?

_____

_____

_____

Think back to a particularly painful experience in your life. Were you able to find any joy in your circumstances at the time? If not, can you identify any sense of joy that may have existed if you view the situation from a different vantage point now?

_____

_____

_____

Actions

Think of a past trial that stretched you in some way. Thank God for the growth that you experienced as a result of that trial.

_____

_____

_____

Pinpoint something you are going through right now that feels incredibly heavy in your life. Pray that God will allow you to experience the presence of joy in and through this situation.

_____

_____

_____

Chapter 6

The Golden Handcuffs

ENERGY ACCOUNT	
DEPOSIT	**WITHDRAWAL**
Motivated by a Healthy Passion for Others	*Motivated by a Healthy Paycheck for Ourselves*

When it comes to understanding our sincere motivations, we need to be honest about how we choose to spend our time and money. We put our largest amount of energy, finances, and efforts into our most coveted longings. Of the three, time is actually the single best indicator of where our heart's desires truly lie. Unfortunately, most of us find ourselves fixated on spending our time striving for that higher salary because our passion for things ranks higher than our passion for our true calling in life—a calling to live modestly and serve others with the resources that are bestowed to us.

Now, if you're working overtime to pay off a medical bill or to keep your family afloat during some trying stretch in your life that wasn't due to your poor decisions (or maybe it was but you've learned from your mistakes and you're trying to right the ship), this is a far cry from what I'm talking about. Sometimes we endure extenuating circumstances, and we are forced to choose a challenging path for some snapshot in time. This is circumstantial, it's not a mindset. What I want to cover is a heart matter.

The "Golden Handcuffs" is a term coined as a strategy for companies to recruit and retain key talent through the offer of incentives they can't refuse. Intrinsically, this is not wrong, and it's actually a win-win for both parties. But I think this concept stretches beyond the negotiation process within the business world. Money and status are often two kings that erroneously sit on the throne of our self-worth, and they drive the decisions we make.

The thought process of "I'll buy this now and pay for it later" or "I'll sacrifice my time to claim the type of income and title that will make me feel complete" becomes an addiction of sorts. We dig a black hole of debt financially or we build up our annual incomes to a point that enslaves us to continue to make more so we can buy more, be more, feel like we've got it all, and keep up with the proverbial Joneses. Yet, we are empty on the inside because attempting to find our meaning by way of personal gain will never be enough. Our efforts start to feel shallow and our spirits take on a heaviness if we dare to honestly assess how our days are spent and why we spend them the way that we do.

Tricia Goyer, the author of *Walk It Out*, puts so much of this in perspective as she uses her book as a battle cry for us to find our full purpose in Christ alone. In her chapter "The Work You're Meant to Do," she writes:

> Remember when you were little and someone asked you, "What do you want to be when you grow up?" It's adorable when six-year-olds say things such as police officer, ballerina, astronaut, or president of the United States. But during high school, most of us settle on a more realistic career choice than POTUS. We evaluate our interests and strengths. We weigh the cost of college and studying, and settle on a career path. Like most of the decisions we make at that age, this choice usually centers on our own happiness.
>
> As we mature, we realize life isn't just about us. Maybe, just maybe, God designed us for a purpose that will impact His kingdom. The purpose we all share as Christ-followers is to worship God, love Him, love others, and live a godly life. But God also gave us individual things to do with our unique gifts and talents ... Too often we believe that only some people are called into Christian ministry and

*the rest of us are off the hook, but truthfully, no matter what we do
for work, God called us there to make an impact for His kingdom.*[1]

Whether we are the CEO of a Fortune 500 company, a small
business owner, a cog in the corporate wheel, a teacher, a leader
in a nonprofit organization, a stay-at-home mom, an industrial
worker, an employee at a local church, or any number of other
positions that fall on the spectrum, we are called to make our
choices based on God's lead and then to make each interaction
count accordingly. Sadly, more often than not, this is not the motivation for our occupational selections and we don't view our
current positions as an opportunity to be a shining light in a dark
world. Instead, we focus on what we can *get* from our careers as
opposed to what we can *give*. We utilize these daily interactions
as a platform for ourselves instead of a pulpit for our God.

And do we even realize what we are sacrificing in the process?
We're giving up so many precious moments and memories with
those we love. We're forfeiting the chance to truly fulfill our God-
given reason for walking this earth. We're losing so many opportunities to be a light to those around us. And eventually, and
possibly permanently, we're sacrificing our good health. These
are all energy withdrawals we make in order to crown ourselves
King or Queen of the Hill or pay off the mounting hill of debt
that bought our fleeting "happiness" somewhere along the way.
Sometimes we view our "passion" as the achievement of things
as opposed to the achievement of our purpose. It's a sad misstep
and one that we need to come to terms with *now*.

There's a story in the Bible that explains this so clearly. A
young, wealthy man came to Jesus and asked how he could enter
the kingdom of heaven. Jesus's response shows us how the love
of money is a giant barrier to the softening of our hearts toward
the desires of Christ and the needs of others. Matthew 19:21–24
paints a great picture of how this love of money relates to our
eternal reality:

---

1   Tricia Goyer, *Walk it Out: The Radical Result of Living God's Word One Step at a Time*,
Colorado Springs, David C. Cook, 2017, 179–80.

Jesus said to him, "If you would be perfect, go, sell what you pos-
sess and give to the poor, and you will have treasure in heaven; and
come, follow me." When the young man heard this he went away sor-
rowful, for he had great possessions.

And Jesus said to his disciples, "Truly, I say to you, only with diffi-
culty will a rich person enter the kingdom of heaven. Again I tell you,
it is easier for a camel to go through the eye of a needle than for a rich
person to enter the kingdom of God."

I have a fitting "God Story" of my own to tell as an encouraging addition to this. It's one that actually took place this past week. Brent and I were feeling the heartbreak of the world around us and discussing how we don't have nearly what we used to, but our needs are met. We're also at a crucial point financially as the continuation of his job at the steel mill seems promising right now but the future is uncertain based on how fast the coronavirus spreads and whether or not the mills will sit idle. We realized that worry had started taking over in relation to our confidence in Christ, so we had to press pause and reset.

We concluded that we needed to be a blessing to those who are struggling through the catastrophic, economic effects of Covid-19, and trust that God would work out the rest. For some reason, the amount of $50 kept popping up in my mind, so we bought $50 worth of baby supplies and sent them to our local domestic violence shelter.

Would you believe that *the same day* I received a message from PayPal that someone near and dear to us just felt the need to send us $50 as a way of blessing our family during our time of hardship? I called her immediately and told her that both of our efforts flowed through to bless those precious children in need of diapers, pacifiers, and Tylenol. I hope it also filled the mothers who received the items with a feeling of assurance that they are loved and that their needs matter to a couple of people who don't know them personally but who want to show them God's love just the same.

John Piper, arguably one of the greatest theologians of our time, had some very direct opinions on this specific topic as well. In his book *Don't Waste Your Life*, he explains how the way we view our possessions is an honest reflection of the way we view Christ:

If we look like our lives are devoted to getting and maintaining things, we will look like the world, and that will not make Christ look great. He will look like a religious side-interest that may be useful for escaping hell in the end, but doesn't make much difference in what we live and love here . . .

The issue of money and lifestyle is not a side issue in the Bible. The credibility of Christ in the world hangs on it. Fifteen percent of everything Christ said relates to this topic—more than his teachings on heaven and hell combined.[2]

Our God is so awesome, friends. He will hold fast to his promise to sustain us. Sometimes we are the ones in need of help, and sometimes we are the ones provided with a surplus that we can use to help others. If we can just grasp this one thing, we will experience a freedom like we've never experienced before. Our bank accounts will no longer dictate our actions. We will be able to live with a calming peace that, regardless of how many figures we make, it's *enough* and our attention can be redirected toward how we can be a resource for Christ in the life of someone else.

You see, we are held tightly by the One who loves us beyond our own understanding, and, because of this, we don't need to hold tightly to the financial illusion of security that embodies no actual power. The reality is that we have zero control. So many people throughout history have gone from everything to nothing monetarily in the blink of a stock market crash, a company reorganization, or any other number of unfortunate scenarios, and many of them go into major depressions or even tragically commit suicide. Why? Because they viewed their net worth as synonymous with their actual worth. Others survive on next to nothing and live out their days with a contentment that can only be explained through their identification as a child of God. *Please* realize that you are more than your *stuff.* Give it away and see how it changes the way you view this world. Your energy account will hit a six-figure high!

I promise you, we will know our purpose if we keep our financial focus outward toward the needs of others as opposed to

---

2 John Piper, *Don't Waste Your Life (Redesign)*, Wheaton, IL, Crossway, 2018, 101–03.

an inward focus on the things we covet. This will bring us the feeling of completeness we constantly chase, and it will give us a sense of closure to that gaping hole in each of our hearts that we all crave so deeply to fill. It's not easy, but it's essential, and it will become more natural over time. Give, and give generously. Your treasures will be waiting in heaven and your soul will be at rest here on earth.

Insights

How do you typically view money? Do you see it as a resource meant to meet your needs and wants or as a resource to meet the needs of others?

_____

_____

_____

What are the top three things you spend your money on or give your money to? Why? What about the top three things you spend your time on? Do the motivations behind these two categories seem to coincide?

_____

_____

_____

_____

_____

_____

How has God provided for you when a situation seemed dire? Do you believe he'll do it again?

_____

_____

_____

_____

Actions

Think of a cause that is important to you in some way (church, local animal rescue, domestic violence shelter, food pantry, etc.). Commit to making a donation, whether it be your time, talent, or treasure. If you have a spouse or children, make sure to include them. Take note of how this shifts the focus of your heart, especially if it stretches you beyond the boundaries of your comfort zone.

_____

_____

_____

_____

_____

_____

Chapter 7

Choose Your Tribe Wisely

ENERGY ACCOUNT	
DEPOSIT	**WITHDRAWAL**
Surrounded by Those Who Lift You Up	*Surrounded by Those Who Drag You Down*

Your circle should want you to win. Your circle should clap the loudest when you have good news. If they don't, get a new circle.

~WESLEY SNIPES~

This might be one of the single most important lessons I've learned throughout my life, and it was magnified tenfold when I got sick. It was then that I realized, more than ever, my need for others on this planet. It was also then that I realized who should take up this space. It's amazing how we are so blinded by easy circumstances, but the raw sting of harsh reality can open our eyes to who's in it for the long haul and who's in it for themselves.

I'm competitive by nature; this has always been hardwired deep in my DNA. I would describe myself more as someone who won't hesitate to bare my teeth when needed, but my claws always stay retracted, even at my own expense. I am the type of individual who shudders at the thought of others failing or suffering in any way. It doesn't matter if they've brought it upon themselves or if they have injected some sort of turmoil into my life. I still don't have a tolerance for people in pain, and I avoid being the cause of it if at all possible. It shatters my heart to cut ties with anyone and I have a bad habit of continuing to throw myself on the sword to salvage relationships that are riddled with toxicity.

As someone who has been in sales for almost my entire professional career, I have pretty thick skin. I can typically take rejection well and bounce back rather quickly. I'm able to tolerate those who think highly of themselves in a business situation and can usually shrug it off as it has no long-term bearing on my personal life. What completely deflates me, however, is the rejection felt by someone who is supposed to be supporting me, or the feeling of being belittled by an individual I've trusted to build me up.

Please don't misunderstand me, there's a big difference between receiving honest, helpful, and constructive criticism in love and being a punching bag for someone else's self-esteem. One is motivated by sincere concern for our well-being and the other is embedded in a selfish need for personal elevation. It's imperative that we understand the difference and use this grid to choose our inner circle wisely.

Sometimes when we are young and our biggest problems have shallow roots, we are blinded to the need for fulfilling and uplifting relationships. As time goes on, however, we begin to encounter experiences that drive us to our darkest places. It's in these places that our solid "go-to's" can make or break our ability to heal and move forward healthily. Their advice, their genuine presence in our most vulnerable hour, the strength of their shoulder that we desperately need to cry on, their desire to point us toward Christ in our pain—these factors will matter, and they will either hinder or accelerate our walk through the journey ahead. The Merriam-Webster.com Thesaurus lists synonyms for the word *tribe* as "blood, clan, family, kin, people, stock."[1] We all have a tribe. How this tribe functions and who this tribe consists of is pivotal to our development as people.

---

1   Merriam-Webster.com Thesaurus, s.v. "tribe," Accessed September 23, 2020, https://www.merriam-webster.com/thesaurus/tribe.

To say that my life has been challenging lately is a gross understatement. I'm struggling—bad. Some days, I'm not even confident that I can carry my youngest child down our stairs without falling or make myself a cup of coffee without dropping a minimum of 17 things in the process. Once my coffee is made, sometimes my face is so numb I can't even keep the coffee I'd worked so hard to brew from running out of the left corner of my mouth. I get down, *way* down and that's before 7 a.m. I feel like I fail an infinite amount of times in a single day. I can't keep up with the laundry; I can't keep my house Pinterest perfect; I can't keep the dishes from piling up; I can't accomplish physical activities with my kids the way I want to; I can't, I can't, I can't. These two words play on a loop in my head quite regularly as of late and I start to wonder if I'm more of a burden to my little family than a help.

But then I turn to my tribe. My husband reminds me of the value I bring as his wife and the mother of our three kiddos. He lends me a solid shoulder, soaks up my tears, gently pieces together my broken heart, and quiets my unforgiving self-talk. My family members put up a hedge to fend off my worries, calm my deepest fears, and step in to fill the gaps. My friends, my priceless friends, know me. They've seen my lowest lows and highest highs and they still accept every part of me. They've been through so much with me and they continue to show up time and time again. This aforementioned group of wonderful people point me toward peace, pray for me, dive into the depths with me, and remind me that God is my refuge and strength. I have and will continue to do the same for them. We are a tribe and together we hold each other up in love and truth.

Two types of energy deposits happen in these relationships. We receive various deposits from our tribe, and we gain energy by making positive deposits into their energy accounts as well. It's refreshing, fulfilling, selfless, and it produces a personal growth in us that we couldn't achieve any other way. And these relationships are not happenstance: they are divine intervention. C.S. Lewis describes it so eloquently:

> *"In friendship . . . we think we have chosen our peers. In reality a few years' difference in the dates of our births, a few more miles between*

certain houses, the choice of one university instead of another . . . the accident of a topic being raised or not raised at a first meeting—any of these chances might have kept us apart. But, for a Christian, there are, strictly speaking no chances. A secret Master of Ceremonies has been at work. Christ, who said to the disciples, "Ye have not chosen me, but I have chosen you," can truly say to every group of Christian friends, "You have not chosen one another but I have chosen you for one another." The friendship is not a reward for our discrimination and good taste in finding one another out. It is the instrument by which God reveals to each of us the beauties of all the others."[2]

Our tribes are not a luxury; we need each other. We were created as relational beings and God has given us friendships on earth to sustain us until we realize the reality of heaven. Cherish those who love you most. They are a legitimate godsend.

While I am so fortunate to have my inner circle of those who rejoice when I rejoice and weep when I weep, I've also encountered people who have the opposite effect. I'm not talking about the good friend who is going through a tough spot, who becomes unable to stand with us for a while. That's a completely different scenario that becomes our time to shine in their time of need. We've all been there, and I'm sure there have been seasons of your life where you, too, had a hard time finding the energy to invest in someone in your inner circle. That's just part of human limitations, and it's nowhere near the type of person I'm about to describe. I'm lasered in on the individuals who are only in it for their gain.

We know these types. They are wolves in sheep's clothing. They pretend to care, draw close when it's in their best interest, and disappear as soon as things get messy. They're conveniently unavailable when we need them most, focused on their own gain, and are ready to drop us if something or someone better comes along. They're the first to point out our flaws and the last to celebrate our successes. They are toxic and their poison has no place in our lives. We should pray for them and send them on their way. Do not dwell in their shadows. The sooner you can

---

2 C.S. Lewis, as quoted by Rob Peabody, *Citizen, Your Role in an Alternate Kingdom*, Oxford, Lion Hudson Limited, 2014, 67–8.

release them, the sooner you can stop wasting your resources on a relationship that will never measure up. Stop the energy withdrawal. This type of one-sided interaction serves as one of the most expensive ways to deplete your energy account.

So please, friends, hold tight to those who hold tight to you and let go of the ones who hold tight to their own agenda. It's okay to let them go. Make room for someone better yoked for you in companionship. Don't waste your limited energy on people who selfishly expect it or simply don't value it at all. You wouldn't continue to blow your money on something that doesn't work, would you? Treat your energy the same way. Give and receive, bless and be blessed, fill and be filled. Know that when you've hit your rock bottom, lost a piece of your soul, or found yourself in a place of total despair, you'll have numbers in your phone to call and shoulders to rest your weary head on. God is our ultimate fortress, but he foreknew our need for human interaction, and he's placed a tribe in our lives to help us navigate our paths on this side of heaven. Thank you, God, for my tribe!

Insights

Why do you think God created relationships? What does the word "tribe" mean to you?

_____

_____

_____

_____

_____

In what ways have you been able to serve and be served by these special people in your life?

_____

_____

_____

_____

Actions

Commit to reevaluating relationships that are toxic and single-sided. Create a plan to start pulling away so that you can make room for others who will lift you up instead of tearing you down.

_____

_____

_____

Identify the closest members of your tribe. Before the week is out, let them know how important they are to you, how much you value their presence in your life, and thank them for any specific things they've said or done to be there for you. You can do this in the form of a text, card, phone call, gift basket, coffee date—be creative and enjoy this opportunity to surprise them with some extra love!

_____

_____

_____

_____

_____

_____

_____

Chapter 8

The State of Your Bodily Temple

ENERGY ACCOUNT	
DEPOSIT	**WITHDRAWAL**
The Boost That Comes from Christ-Focused Upkeep	*The Drain That Comes from Trashing the Place or Idolizing Its Exterior*

> *Do you not know that your body is a temple of the*
> *Holy Spirit within you, whom you have from God?*
> *You are not your own, for you were bought*
> *with a price. So glorify God in your body.*
> ~1 CORINTHIANS 6:19–20~

This is a subject that most of us feel tugging at our heartstrings, but it's not one we want to dive into too deeply because we're afraid of the conviction we might find under the surface. God reminds us in his Word that our bodies are not to be used for self-indulgence or self-annihilation. Instead, they are to be utilized in a way that creates proper housing for the Holy Spirit. That sounds peachy on paper, but the accomplishment of this takes a level of dedication and discipline that we can't produce on our own. It gets down to a gut level that separates the "what" from the "why." This is the point where we start to get squirmy and dodgy and where we need to lean on Christ for direction and change.

In case you need a quick reminder, we're human. As such, we're also typically surrounded by a plethora of nasty sins that make every effort to invade our hearts and justify our actions. One of the easiest ways for Satan to infiltrate our energy accounts is through the misuse of the physical vessel we have been given to cherish and guard exclusively for the honor of our King. When it comes to transgressions involving our bodies, we can bend to one of two extremes or fluctuate along the line of this unhealthy spectrum. At one end is the creation of an idol as we place so much focus and effort on our figure and overall appearance that our image becomes our addiction. At the other end, we don't respect our bodies at all and abuse them with things like casual sex, drugs, alcohol, chain smoking, eating disorders, gluttony, lack of exercise, or a general attitude of not giving a rip.

This is really tough, you guys. We live in a world flashing all kinds of mixed messages at us in rapid succession. Hollywood tends to make drunkenness and one-night stands seem like an innocent staple in our society, the media often glamorizes lifestyles riddled with all kinds of unhealthy habits that don't seem to lead to any negative consequences, and advertising flaunts half-naked models with flawless figures stuffing their mouths with whatever junk food they're attempting to sell. We are encouraged to believe the lie that this gift we are given is ours to treat however we selfishly see fit. The problem with this is that it's not why we were created and, as we know, using things for purposes other than how they were meant to be used often causes them to malfunction and eventually break altogether.

When we put too much effort into perfecting our bodies in the name of vanity, we may superficially feel alive, but we are depleting our energy accounts, nonetheless. You see, our fine-tuned shapes might seem impressive, but our deflated spirits will feel unsettled from the conviction of our true intentions. When we maintain our bodies to serve our egos, our souls will become restless and empty. We may appear healthy and happy to those around us, but the anchor of insecurity will grow increasingly heavy and it will eventually drag our spiritual energy down— exhausting any physical energy we've gained in the course of our futile efforts. And at some point, we will begin to realize that the aging process is inevitable. Imperfections are bound to creep in. Our attempts at maintaining a youthful exterior will start to feel fruitless, and we'll have to face the reality that the worth we worked so hard to acquire is embedded in our outward shell instead of our inward service to the Lord.

While some fall into the first category of idolizing their bodies, there's another group that either simply doesn't care too much about physical well-being or has an underlying emotional issue manifesting itself in the form of physical neglect. If you find yourself in this crowd, one explanation could be that you don't hold your health in high regard, and you'd prefer to enjoy what you want when you want as opposed to exerting discipline and self-control. However, that temporary enjoyment is not worth the long-term damaging effects your body will experience as a result of your negative choices.

Another possibly more prominent reason to take up a seat in this self-destructive boat has to do with stuffing down something difficult and replacing it with some sort of unhealthy distraction instead of turning to Christ for relief and support. You find that you tend to withdraw from your energy account by harming your body through substance abuse, poor nutrition, lack of exercise, reckless promiscuity, etc. You use something damaging to mask the real pain that you don't have the energy to deal with, but you'll always find yourself in this state of energy deficit if you keep repeating the poison of your choice. This cycle is a hard one to break as each bad decision turns into a bad habit that then becomes more of a lifestyle than a string of things we opt in or out of.

Sometimes we don't quite fit into either of these categories. Sometimes our bodies just plain fail us. Joints become damaged, cancer invades our cells, mental and emotional disorders play a game of "tug of war" with our minds, and chronic illness causes fatigue. We find ourselves more sedentary than we used to be, and there are only a limited number of options we have to cope in these situations. Someone who struggles with a bad leg cannot realistically be expected to run a marathon. Grace and patience must live with us in this space. We have to trust that God has allowed our challenges for a reason and that he also has the desire to equip us with peace and mercy to endure this season in a way that pleases him.

Regarding all of the above, there is no judgment here, friends. I've fallen into each of these three categories at various points in my life. Roughly fifteen years ago, I went through an extremely challenging time in my life and I found myself too stressed out to eat. As a result, I began dropping sizes faster than a Cy Young pitcher drops a curveball and I started to feel my confidence grow as my waistline shrank. To keep the pounds off, I ate far too few calories and exercised excessively. My view of a healthy body was completely distorted. I'm thankful that God changed my mindset and helped me see that while a nutritious diet and sensible exercise routine are within his plan, going about these things in a way that was both unhealthy and glorifying myself negated any true spiritual value. I was trading my outward appearance for my inward soul.

Somehow over the years, I went from someone who lost my appetite in the face of affliction to someone who started eating my feelings. I would binge on a bag of whatever was handy in order to avoid having to experience emotional discomfort. I already have a hard time keeping weight off under normal circumstances; hand me a cheeseburger and I'll gain five pounds simply from looking at it. If I go beyond my allotted calories for the day, I know I will pay for it when I step on the scale.

This became a constant war zone for me as I started turning to food for comfort instead of turning to Christ. I wasn't making choices that were right for my body or my spirit. Instead, I was making decisions that self-soothed whatever emotional or physical pain I was feeling. I'd have a bad day and eat a container of ice cream instead of asking the Lord for comfort. I'd have trouble shutting my brain off at night so I would down a few sleeping pills instead of praying for peace. I was not viewing my body as a temple for the Holy Spirit; I was viewing it as mine to use and abuse however I wanted to.

In the last few years, my body has experienced challenges outside of my control. These physical ailments have caused me to become more immobile and increasingly frustrated as I struggle to do things the same way I used to. My physical activity is minimized, my diet has changed due to foods that trigger my attacks, my weight has yo-yoed as one medication that suppressed my appetite was replaced by one that made me feel hungry all the time, and another medicine caused my hair to fall out in small chunks for a while. My face has a slight droop, my left side doesn't fully function as it should, both knees are going out, and, if I'm not incredibly careful, my chronic illnesses continue to rear their ugly heads.

I thank God every day for Brent who has loved me through every bodily change. I know there are times I'm not the most attractive physically or emotionally. The things that are beyond my control are the ones that gnaw at me the most. The other two stages of my life were hard, but I knew I could rely on the strength of God to place me back on the course of physical health. It's not that he can't heal the things I'm facing now, it's just that I don't know if he will. This has been, by far, the hardest season for me to accept but it's also the one that's produced the most amount of growth. I'm becoming more comfortable in the body I've been given and focusing my efforts inward as I make every attempt to declutter my heart and provide a proper place for the Holy Spirit to dwell.

I'm not sure where you land on this continuum, but I do know two things to be true of all of us—we are called to be a temple and our temples are "fixer-uppers" in progress. The ideal goal is for our bodies to be suitable dwelling places for the Holy Spirit to live within us. Let me help you visualize what this looks like. My brother recently had two of his dear friends and their sweet, little baby stay with him when they came into town. Now, my brother is a bachelor in his early 30s. His spare bedroom served as an office/storage area. He knew this setup was not good enough for his special guests to reside in. They are important to him, and he wanted to make sure they were comfortable and cared for. He gave the room a total makeover, moving his stuff out and setting up a cozy bedroom in its place—he even went above and beyond by purchasing brand new sheets and pillows to make sure they could get the best sleep possible. When you sincerely care about someone, you go the extra mile to set your things aside and make room for the ones you love.

We need to move our junk out of the way and make an acceptable spot for the Holy Spirit to settle in. We won't do this impeccably in this lifetime; we can't because we will struggle with a sin nature until we step into eternity. We are in a state of much-needed TLC and that's where God comes in with a wet mop and a fresh coat of paint. He takes our willingness to commit our lives to him and begins working on us one project at a time.

As we start to incorporate drinking more water, embracing a healthier diet, and sticking to a realistic exercise routine, we'll no doubt make sizeable deposits into our energy accounts. But it's about more than that. It's about our "why" in this particular category. The justification for our actions should take the focus off of our own desires and place it on desiring to be a worthy host or hostess to the Holy Ghost. Once we can fully adopt this line of thinking, we can have faith that the Lord has the ability and longing to remodel us from the ground up. All we have to do is hand him our hammer—he's already provided the nails.

Insights

Which category do you currently fall in as it relates to your body—are you idolizing it, abusing it, struggling with conditions beyond your control, or some combination of the three? Are you willing to release these challenges to the Lord and allow yourself to be renovated in Christ?

_____

_____

_____

_____

_____

What are some healthy physical, spiritual, and emotional habits you've formed in your life? What are some unhealthy ones?

_____

_____

_____

_____

_____

Actions

Now that you've identified certain unhealthy habits in the question above, think through some ways you can start to refocus your health goals around the Holy Spirit and, in turn, undo these habits. Ask God to help you stop where you are and start moving in a healthy direction.

_____

_____

_____

_____

_____

We have all done things in the past that have grieved the Holy Spirit. If you haven't already, ask him for forgiveness in these areas and for an ability to move forward.

_____

_____

_____

_____

_____

Know that being "under construction" doesn't render you useless. Pray for the Lord to show you opportunities in which you can be a part of someone else's growth as you continue to experience your own.

_____

_____

_____

_____

_____

Chapter 1

There's a Freedom in Honesty

ENERGY ACCOUNT	
DEPOSIT	**WITHDRAWAL**
The Release That Comes with Owning Reality	*The Price That Comes with Pretending*

Facebook. Twitter. Instagram. Pinterest. TikTok. Snapchat . . . pick your social platform poison. It doesn't matter which one; they are all chock-full of fake smiles, embellished excursions, and masked mayhem. Let me clarify that I'm not suggesting we air every load of dirty laundry for the entire Internet to witness or that it's wrong to share a nice photo of your family dipping your toes in the Pacific. Obviously, some things need to remain private and some things express honest enjoyment. But too many of us feel this pressure to appear in a state of perfection at all times, and we go to weird lengths to paint a portrait of the opposite of our reality simply to keep up a nice visual of a false existence.

There are a ton of problems with this, but I would like to high-light the two that I think are the most damaging. The first is the pressure to keep up the lie. Yes, I said *lie*. If your marriage isn't fantastic, you don't need to smear it all over the World Wide Web. But going overboard with the "I love my spouse; he's my best friend forever" posts makes it tough to face people in person when it's becoming increasingly obvious that your relationship is strained. Pretending things are what they're not only raises this invisible bar that you're constantly trying to chin up to. It also causes you to fall harder and hit the ground with a more painful blow when all is exposed in time. This will make consistent and significant withdrawals from your energy account each time you have to keep up the façade. It will become exhausting— trust me, I know firsthand.

The second problem is that "perfect people" become roped off from imperfect people, and they are the last ones we are able to connect with on any sort of meaningful level. Your pain has a purpose. Let me repeat that so you hear me loud and clear . . . *your pain has a purpose!* Your devastating and life-altering experiences make you raw, yes, but they also make you relatable. Sympathy is an important quality, but it can only go so far. It takes someone who has walked through the same deep valley you have to accurately understand your hurts, your fears, your scars, and your frustrations.

The key to these connections, however, is reliant on honesty. An authentic transparency of the struggles in your life may strike a chord in someone who is sinking in the same boat. Connections are made, friendships are forged, feelings of profound understanding take place. It's a wonderful byproduct of tragedy, and it makes deposits into your energy account whether you are on the giving or receiving end of this extended kindness and first-hand compassion.

I've played this game many times. I've pretended life was paradise when bombs were going off all around me. I've lived through years of constant heartache while simultaneously using every ounce of my energy to convince everyone that things couldn't be better. I was able to keep this up for a while because I was offsetting my energy account withdrawals with temporary deposits made through career successes. These weren't equal tradeoffs, but they were like a partially-deflated life raft that just barely kept my head above water (functional in the moment, but destined for disaster).

I developed a distinct talent for masking my anguish so well that when I announced my divorce after my first marriage of 10 trying years, people were completely shocked. Now, was it necessary to share some of the messy details with everyone I encountered? Absolutely not. But instead of coming to terms with reality, I painted a picture that I convinced everyone to view through rose-colored glasses. I set the stage as one of a happy home with happy people and a happy future. None of it was true and I paid with my energy account for each false impression.

Fast forward to my new chapter in life that bloomed almost six years ago. I met, fell head over heels for, and happily married Brent (all in the span of three and half months—yes you read that correctly!). I pushed my career to the next tier, had two kids in two years, and juggled so many balls that I swear I should have won some world record. Obviously, I'm not one to take things slow.

I would travel to my customers all over the country while taking phone calls from home about how my daughter hit her head at school, my son had a high fever, or the baby just took her first steps. I would get off a plane after three days of a conference in another time zone, drive the two and a half hours home from the airport in rush-hour traffic, make dinner for my family, and then run my daughter to soccer practice (all of this by my choice). I wasn't sleeping. I wasn't focusing on any aspect of my health: physical, mental, spiritual, or otherwise. I was drowning and I knew it.

If you would ask me how I was doing, I was freaking fantastic! Superwoman in heels, baby, living the social media dream while wasting away behind the scenes. I loved the high of constant motion, and I hated turning down any chance to prove myself, so I just kept piling it on even though I felt the cracks forming. I presented a polished exterior, but I silently felt myself falling apart one small piece at a time.

Listen to me closely. If you take nothing else away from reading these pages, I want you to grasp this one thing. You are not made to be all things to all people. If you try, you *will* break. I broke, you guys. And I broke in a way that was beyond fixing physically. When I hit the ground, I hit it with full force and it *hurt*! It was a pain I'm still not able to get past. It was the tragic and sudden end to a big part of my life that left me feeling alone, scared, frustrated, and angrier at myself than I had ever been.

And to top it off, would you believe I hid my physical symptoms from almost everyone around me for over a year? I pushed past every warning sign and presented myself as someone not only surviving but thriving. If I had a quarter for how many times people told me they "didn't know how I did it all," I'd have a healthy chunk of dough. The truth was I wasn't doing it all—not well, anyway—but I had gotten quite good at making it appear as though I was unfazed and unscathed by the constant chaos controlling my life.

And why? For what? Well, pride was my main motivation. I started to realize that maybe I had bitten off a bit more than I could chew in everything I was committing to—but admitting that was something I simply wasn't willing to do. I longed for the husband I now called mine, I prayed for the three children that I covered in kisses every chance I got, I hoped for the kind of career I was now excelling at, I desired to be there for every friend and family member who needed to chat. In addition, I tried to fit in the gym at least two times a week, manage our household, attend every event I was invited to, and maybe fit in a hobby or two. None of these life building blocks was wrong in its own right, but I don't know anyone who could stack all of these up at once without the whole tower toppling over. Yet, somehow, I was sure I was different, stronger, more equipped to push beyond healthy boundaries. Spoiler alert: I wasn't.

Another reason was rooted in the fact that I hate the thought of disappointing anyone. The thing that motivates me more than money, more than a fancy title, more than the possibility of moving up through the socioeconomic ranks, is the satisfaction of knowing that I'm useful, dependable, consistent. I want so badly to be the person that everyone can rely on, the one who will raise their hand to help and drop all of my needs for a chance to shine for someone else. There's nothing fundamentally wrong with wanting to be helpful, but there's a balance that has to take place, and my scale was tipped full tilt in the wrong direction.

A third prominent reason was that I genuinely love to work, and I equally loved my job—the people, the challenges, the experiences, the company itself. It suited me, and I honestly looked forward to Mondays (weird, I know). I still sincerely miss so much of my former career and I think I always will to some extent. I spoke to a dear friend about the feelings of loss I was experiencing, and she wisely told me that I would need to treat this no differently than a physical death. Whoa. Talk about stopping you in your tracks. A huge part of my identity had died. I had to be honest with myself about the fact that things had changed and that I had wrapped so much of myself up in what I did for a living. I had to face it and I had to grieve it.

So, back to the "do it all" attitude that I fought so hard to hold on to so I could keep up with appearances. Regardless of my reasons, I was withdrawing my energy account at a rapid pace with no time or resources to replenish it. I was flat out overspending. Once I blew through my entire energy balance, I started borrowing with interest. I got so far into energy debt that there was no way to come back out of it without claiming physical bankruptcy and starting over with the scraps of myself that remained. Knowing that I'll probably never be one hundred percent of my former self again is certainly jolting, but it's also what forced me to come clean about what was going on.

This wake-up call was so pivotal. God finally forced me to be still in a way I couldn't fight against. I actually tried to go back to work after taking a short medical leave and God allowed two more nasty health episodes to sit me right back down. Was I angry? Yep. Did I have *several* questions for God? You bet. But I knew it also saved my quality of life. The race I was running was an impossible one to win. My physical, mental, emotional, and spiritual health were all at stake, and keeping this trial completely undercover made it that much harder to endure. How many times could I say, "I'm fine," when I'm having one of the hardest seasons of my life? How many excuses could I come up with for not attending anything in person before 9 a.m. because my left side took that long to start working properly every morning? How many ways could I try to explain away my odd symptoms? Can you relate? It's awful and it's not a cross we're meant to bear alone—*ever*.

One of the defining moments in my journey thus far was when I announced to everyone on social media that I was, in fact, not okay. I was terrified, humbled, and I felt emotionally naked. I wrote my sentences so many times over, prayed for the right words, deleted, edited, wrestled with second thoughts. Was this the right move? Should I expose myself to this magnitude? It took everything in me to hit the "post" button, but it had to be done. I couldn't hide any longer, nor did I want to. It wasn't fair to me or my family and God had bigger plans for my pain.

Here were my actual words:

WE NEED YOUR PRAYER FRIENDS

Since I had Gwyn a year ago, I knew something wasn't right with my body. At first I thought I just needed more time to bounce back than I did with my other two kiddos (gotta love a "geriatric pregnancy") and I had some anemia and other vitamin deficiencies so we attributed a lot of my early symptoms to these factors. But after several months of progressively worse symptoms I knew something wasn't right. I ended up in the hospital three times since Gwyn was born—once for postpartum preeclampsia where I also experienced mild facial paralysis and twice for (what we thought was) Bell's palsy months later. I've also been through numerous doctors and tests these last 12 months.

I've been fairly quiet about it over this past year because I could hide it pretty well and we kept thinking it would get better. This is no longer the case. I've got paresthesia and neuropathy throughout my left side: in my face, hand, arm, and foot. I've lost some of my function in my left hand, my left arm is fatigued, and my left leg/foot is starting to experience some weakness as well. I've got memory loss, brain fog, dizziness, fatigue . . . the list goes on.

So, we're humbly asking, will you pray for us? We are struggling. I'm physically unable to keep up, Brent is trying his best, but as you can imagine, three kids and two hectic work schedules have pushed us to our limits (beyond, if we're being honest). Our families and close friends have helped fill the gaps, for which we are so thankful. But we are still young in this journey. There are more tests, more specialists, more answers to be sought. It's starting to look like this might be a bit more grueling than we originally hoped. And through it all we're trying so hard to keep life as normal as possible for our sweet babies. We would so welcome being covered in prayer right now—we need it more than we ever have.

Once it was out there, I held my breath. What will others think of me now? The vulnerability of this single act had my heart beating a million miles a minute. But then something incredible happened. I began getting private messages and texts from people I had no clue were wrestling with their own versions of despair. Somehow, with the push of a button, my confession made my struggle real, and I became someone worth confiding in. My simple act of honesty gave others the courage to do the same. Isn't it crazy how God works in the form of irony? The things we fear the most oftentimes become our biggest wins in the end, and it's the step of honesty that makes this transition possible.

> *Your greatest test is when you are to bless someone else*
> *while you are going through your own storms.*
> ~UNKNOWN~

Take off the mask, my friend. You can't breathe under there. You're slowly suffocating yourself and stunting your ability to heal and grow. You're also cutting your heart off from something special that can come from your battles. When tragedy can lead to triumph through the act of coming alongside someone in a similar situation, you can experience an energy account deposit like you've never had before. In a moment, you go from feeling completely isolated to feeling your sorrow might be the Lord's way of using you as an inspiration for someone else's hope.

Insights

In what ways are you trying to mask some of the struggles in your life?

_____

_____

_____

Do you find it easier to confide in someone when you know they can relate because they've been in the trenches, too?

_____

_____

When you've been brave enough to be vulnerable, have you found that it's allowed others to open up to you about their pain as well?

_____

_____

_____

Actions

Take some time to reflect on how much energy you're using to hide your hurts. Evaluate the energy deposit you would make even if you only confided in one or two people.

_____

_____

_____

_____

_____

Ask God to make a way for you to be someone's beacon of hope. Request that he uses a trial you have faced or are currently facing to allow you to pour love into someone enduring something similar. Take note of how that makes you feel both about the person you've connected with and to God himself.

_____

_____

_____

_____

_____

Chapter 10

The Isolation of Pain and the Gravity of Grace

ENERGY ACCOUNT	
DEPOSIT	**WITHDRAWAL**
Working through Your Hang-Ups with an Attitude of Grace	*Walking through Your Heartache with a Lone Wolf Mentality*

> *God's mercy and grace give me hope—*
> *for myself and for our world.*[1]
> ~BILLY GRAHAM~

This chapter is being written with raw emotion and honesty (I'm applying the principles of Chapter 9!). It's not because the rest of these chapters aren't directly from my heart; it has more to do with the fact that I'm currently in a state of a "Grade A," deep-seated funk. Today has not been a great day. In the interest of transparency, I'm coming at this from a place of genuine angst. I had yet another doctor's appointment (which I'm getting quite tired of, frankly), and I've spent a good chunk of the remainder of the day dealing with all of the fun things that come along with navigating ongoing medical anarchy (please note my

---

1 Billy Graham, as quoted by John Charles Pollock, *The Billy Graham Story*, Grand Rapids, MI, Zondervan, 2011, 131.

not-so-subtle sarcasm, a natural side effect of my aforementioned bad attitude).

To say I'm "in a mood" is an understatement. I've been short-tempered with my kids and my husband most of the afternoon, I've been binge-eating chocolate and carbs like it's my full-time job, and I'm not going to admit to you what time I started drinking a glass of cabernet. I was over this day before it even got started. I hate feeling like this—no I *loathe* feeling like this—which kicks my anger into overdrive, which triggers my guilt, which makes me that much angrier, and the cycle continues.

Ugh, I just want to go to bed and start over. If only that were an option. I bet we would all jump at the chance to use a free pass to get out of the jail cell labeled "regret." I'm guessing you've had a moment or two like this as well: stretches of agony in your life where you felt no one around you could understand; you were alone in your pain and there was no way someone could possibly understand the inner workings of your heartache. While there's an ounce of truth to this, the result is, sadly, more loneliness. Deep gashes have an incredibly cruel and impeccably effective way of pulling us apart from the pack, whether it's through a heavy feeling we can't adequately express, an experience we believe no one else can relate to, or the fact that we just don't have the mental energy to try to explain the details of whatever it is that's crushing our soul.

Ironically, today also happens to be Good Friday. Our pastor's sermon related the current isolation of Covid-19 to the devastating separation Jesus felt from his Father on the cross. Admittedly, I was in no mood to stream the service (this is what we have resorted to these days due to mandatory social distancing). Despite my desire to avoid anything holy, my husband and I attempted to start watching it twice only to get interrupted by our kids' lack of ability to stay entertained and my pure lack of motivation in general. Finally, late into the evening, we turned it on and, man, did I need to hear that message. It's funny how it always seems to work out this way. Satan and God both know our needs. While the devil throws every distraction our way, the Lord's persistence remains steady and true.

It was just hours ago that I was crying to Brent about how

alone I feel in my ongoing health drama. I know people care and sincerely try to help, but there's just this stubborn part of me that can't seem to let go of the fact that they'll never get it. No one can possibly understand the depth of my pain, right? How could they unless they were somehow able to pull a "Freaky Friday" switch and live my life for a few days (or a few years to get a more accurate account)? I just want to limp away like a wounded animal and hide in some dark cave, left alone to tend to all the things that are causing me discomfort and distress.

But then I was slapped square in the face by Jesus' words on the cross, "My God, my God, why have you forsaken me?" (Matthew 27:46). No one else in the history of the human race will ever feel the weight of the world, while simultaneously feeling the absence of his Father (from whom he had never been separated). And yet Jesus accepted this pain willingly and lovingly even though he knew how horrible the journey would be. At any moment he could have left us to our own hell-bound devices while he went back to paradise. But he didn't. His grace was greater than his pain.

This is my heart's desire for both myself and for those who are reading this. May our grace also be greater than our pain. I'm hurting from multiple angles, but grace toward others who are trying to understand will make increasingly significant deposits into my energy account instead of the withdrawals caused by an erroneous sense that I'm always going it alone. Will anyone ever be able to fully grasp my exact feelings and thoughts? Of course not, except for Jesus himself. He foreknew our trials before they existed. Our Savior took every single heartache with him to Calvary, and he claimed victory over all of it for us so we would be spared the ultimate pain of eternal separation from God. Grace was defined in that moment and patterned for us to follow in the footsteps of the one who blazed the trail with his own blood.

Every lonely tear, every frustrated word I wish I could take back, every begging question I may never find the answer to on this side of heaven—Jesus understood all of it perfectly and extended grace for every last bit of it. Because of his pain, I can extend grace in my pain, too. This will be an internal struggle for me for a while, no doubt. The mental pity parties I've thrown myself have been epic, but this false sense of validation to fly solo costs me dearly once my moment of fleeting relief disappears. The expense of my private "poor me" sessions will always result in the depletion of my energy account once the dust truly settles and I'm left feeling more alone than before and with less energy to cope. Sarah Walton said it well in her cowritten book, *Hope When It Hurts*: "Contentment is in the presence of Christ, and not in the absence of pain."[2]

Choose grace, friends. There's a gravity to it, a weight that keeps our feet on the ground and our attitudes in check toward the desires of God. It takes our internal attitude of pushing people away and turns it back out toward drawing those in who mean well in their efforts. None of us can entirely relate to each other's battles, but we can do our best to dress the wounds we are allowed to see. Jesus is the only one looking through a lens that isn't skewed or distorted. He has the distinct advantage of knowing the full picture of our hearts better than we know them ourselves. He desires that we do our absolute best to love one another the same way he loved us and continues to show us his divine mercy.

All too often we get this twisted around and expect others to love us the way we love ourselves. This is not at all how life is meant to work, and fighting against the way we were designed to function will only create more days like I experienced today. It's draining, it's regretful and, to put it bluntly, it's sin.

I detest these days, you guys. I muddle through wishing the entire 24 hours away. I'm inward-focused, outwardly hostile, and incredibly short-tempered. I go to bed feeling defeated while making a mental checklist of who I need to apologize to in the morning. It's an awful complexity that just adds another heavy layer of sadness and remorse to my already hurting heart, not to mention that now I've hurt the hearts of others as well. I come bearing my apologies with my head hung low and something amazing happens. Often, I experience the grace of those I had wronged, and I'm humbly reminded of how that feels, too. The heaviness lifts

---

2   Sarah Walton and Kristen Wetherell, *Hope When it Hurts: Biblical Reflections to Help You Grasp God's Purpose in Your Suffering*, Charlotte, NC, Good Book Company, 2017, 158.

and I begin to reexamine my mindset. The self-indulgence of the lone wolf mentality isn't worth the price we pay for it in the end. The gravity of grace, on the other hand, is a wise investment in both ourselves and those around us. It will multiply with interest and we'll be eternally grateful for the fruit it will bear.

Insights

Is there anything you're going through right now that you feel no one else can fully understand?

_____

_____

_____

_____

_____

When you are hurting, do you open your heart to others, or do you tend to retreat into your pain? Why?

_____

_____

_____

_____

_____

Actions

Spend some time in prayer crying out to your heavenly Father. Ask him to make his presence known to you in your time of pain and to give you a sense of peace in the midst of your sorrow. Acknowledge that he truly gets every ounce of agony that you're going through.

_____

_____

_____

This week, commit to working on extending grace to others who are not walking the same path you are but who are trying their best to relate and help as much as they know how.

_____

_____

_____

Chapter 11

The Funny Thing about Fear

ENERGY ACCOUNT	
DEPOSIT	**WITHDRAWAL**
A Faith That Claims Victory over Unhealthy Fear	*A Paralyzing Belief in Our Own Power over Circumstances*

As I'm writing this, we are smack dab in the middle of a global pandemic that has changed life as we know it. A sense of fear is something everyone understands right now. I have also experienced my own challenge with fear as it relates to my health, and I lived in a constant state of crisis for far too long which only worsened my condition on all levels.

See, the funny thing about fear is that while it causes us to recoil as if to offer some protection from the threat of smoke, it is by its very nature an accelerant on the harmful flames. It's the fuel poured onto the already burning fire that causes a moderate spark to become a blazing inferno. I want to be clear that I'm not talking about healthy fears that, I believe, are God-given and keep us away from situations we have no business being around. Please heed these divine warnings and run quickly in the opposite direction. I'm talking about the fear of unknown situations that result in us becoming paralyzed, frozen in our own "what-ifs."

You guys, we do not sit at the control panel of our lives, no matter how much we want to believe we do. We worry because we think fearing the unknown has value, but it doesn't; it only causes more unhealthy anxiety. According to John 10:10, Jesus says, "The thief comes only to steal and kill and destroy. I came that they may have life and have it abundantly."

Irrational fear is a thief, and it infiltrates our minds at the hands of the devil. It steals our joy, our hope, and our faith. God has purposed us to live a life free of this tormenting bondage. Trials are meant to strengthen us in this life and allow us opportunities to build up treasures in our eternal home. This is not an easy concept to accept and I will probably always wrestle with it to some extent. In fact, I'm still battling to find complete acceptance in my health journey, but the closer I get to trusting that the Lord has this handled, the more each obstacle in my life seems to make sense.

I started out with so many questions about what in the world I was even suffering from. I'm still facing questions today, including what this will mean for my future. Will this eventually lead to something more debilitating if I continue to allow the intensity of my stress to get too high? Will I be on all of these medications for the rest of my life? Will my chronic conditions worsen despite my best efforts? Will I ever get to a point where I completely accept my new path and quit holding on so tightly to the previous version of myself?

This is so tough, friends. I don't know if I'll ever really get it all sorted out on this side of heaven, but I'm giving it my best shot. And you know what? Each positive step I take forward comes with a peace that really does pass all understanding. It's a peace that is so incredibly freeing! I'm no longer trapped in the bondage of feeling like I'm somehow responsible for navigating a ship being tossed at sea when the helm isn't anywhere within my reach. Sure, I can seek out the best doctors and take the right medications, but, in the end, God's hand is guiding my vessel. He's laying the foundation for where all of this will lead, and my one and only job is to trust that he is doing it in love.

Second Timothy 1:7 tells us, "God gave us a spirit not of fear but of power and love and self-control." I want to break this verse down as I believe it is chock-full of so much good truth! First of all, it starts with explaining that three of these qualities are from God and one is not. As mentioned before, a healthy sense of fear in the context of a "don't touch the hot stove" situation is in no way a sin. In fact, it is a sign of Christian wisdom. What this passage is referring to is a spirit of fear. This is a chronic state of living that revolves every scenario around a fearful attitude. Every decision, every circumstance, every element of life that seems outside of our control, causes mental, physical, emotional, and spiritual paralysis and panic. This is no way to live. This is prison.

When I began my medical journey, I had no answers, no idea what to expect, and no end in sight. I started thinking of every possible worst-case scenario, I searched the Internet for every symptom, and I tried every natural remedy I could get my hands on. I became obsessed and it only made me worse. What I kept failing to realize was that God was fully in charge of each cell in my body the entire time. He was tenderly nudging me to let go knowing full well that there was no way I would land anywhere but in the palm of his caring hand. He knew he had me covered; he was just helping me to know it, too.

C.S. Lewis had an incredible perspective when it came to the paralyzing nature of fear:

> In one way we think a great deal too much of the atomic bomb. "How are we to live in an atomic age?" I am tempted to reply: "Why, as you would have lived in the sixteenth century when the plague visited London almost every year, or as you would have lived in a Viking age when raiders from Scandinavia might land and cut your throat any night; or indeed, as you are already living in an age of cancer, an age of syphilis, an age of paralysis, an age of air raids, an age of railway accidents, an age of motor accidents."
>
> In other words, do not let us begin by exaggerating the novelty of our situation. Believe me, dear sir or madam, you and all whom you love were already sentenced to death before the atomic bomb was invented: and quite a high percentage of us were going to die in unpleasant ways. We had, indeed, one very great advantage over our ancestors—anesthetics; but we have that still. It is perfectly ridiculous to go about whimpering and drawing long faces because

the scientists have added one more chance of painful and premature death to a world which already bristled with such chances and in which death itself was not a chance at all, but a certainty.

This is the first point to be made: and the first action to be taken is to pull ourselves together. If we are all going to be destroyed by an atomic bomb, let that bomb when it comes find us doing sensible and human things—praying, working, teaching, reading, listening to music, bathing the children, playing tennis, chatting to our friends over a pint and a game of darts—not huddled together like frightened sheep and thinking about bombs. They may break our bodies (a microbe can do that) but they need not dominate our minds.[1]

As we come back to dissecting 2 Timothy 1:7, I find it so curious that nothing in the verse indicates that any of the positive qualities stated were developed by us in any way. These are *gifts* that our loving God has given us as a means to not just survive the scary stuff, but to *thrive* in the midst of it! He doesn't simply *take away* a spirit of fear; he *gives* us a spirit of power, love, and a sound mind. Three for one—that's a pretty incredible exchange! We just have to be open and willing to accepting it.

I thought it would be terrifying to finally let go of the reins, but I was pleasantly surprised to find relief instead. I'm not completely healed physically by any means and there's a rock-solid chance I may never be, but my soul has found the sweet beginnings of the peaceful resolution it needs to mend. I can face each challenge with a renewed sense of confidence knowing that, no matter the outcome, my heavenly Father is working all of this together for good because I love him and I'm called according to his purpose.

So, let go, friends. You won't fall outside of the perfect and affectionate will of your Creator. Quite the opposite. You'll be supported by the omnipotent God of the universe who has gifted you with the tools to face your journey without a spirit of fear. I may not be able to see how my story ends, and some of the pages may not be written exactly how I would have composed them, but the

---

1   C.S. Lewis, "On Living in an Atomic Age," *Present Concerns: A Compelling Collection of Timely, Journalistic Essays*, Orlando, FL, Harcourt Brace Jovanovich, 2002, 73–4.

Writer is holding the pen ever so gently in his fingers and, with a Father's smile, he's composing my chapters with crimson ink flowing from his own sacrifice made out of nothing less than unending love. The details of my destiny have never been in more capable hands and I have never been more grateful.

Insights

What are some areas of your life and future that you fear most?

_____

_____

_____

_____

Think about a time when you feared the worst in a situation. Regardless of whether the worst really happened or nothing bad happened at all, in what ways did your fear specifically deplete your energy account?

_____

_____

_____

_____

Actions

Unnecessary fear is a major stressor on our bodies. Identify at least one current situation that you are facing and pray that you'll find a sense of peace in the unknown. Commit to placing your trust in God to orchestrate the outcome instead of letting fear control your thoughts and emotions.

_____

_____

_____

_____

Chapter 12

Hope in the Darkness

ENERGY ACCOUNT	
DEPOSIT	**WITHDRAWAL**
Bold Faith in the Hope of Christ	*A Need for Our Own 20/20 Vision*

The following is a poem I wrote in the midst of my questions and fears, having no real answers to what was wrong with my body nor where my life would go from this point:

> *Lord, only you can see the answers.*
> *And only through the test of time*
> *Will trust accept that hard disasters*
> *Reveal a Father's love sublime.*
>
> *My faith alone propels me forward*
> *When fear and weakness hold me back.*
> *Eternal hope to carry onward*
> *When strength and sight are what I lack.*
>
> *I know you're here; I feel your presence.*
> *I hear your voice; it calms my sea.*
> *When waves may toss me from my comfort,*
> *You walk on water straight to me.*

I'm thankful that your Word holds power,
A light within this darkened place.
You're by my side and hold me firmly
With loving arms so full of grace.

Though mountains stretch beyond my vision
With clarity outside my view,
I trust you'll lead me through this dessert
To peace and stillness wrapped in you!

Sometimes we have a clear path forward. Sometimes things make absolutely no sense at all, and we feel like we're groping around in the dark for anything solid. The irony is that the clear paths give us a false sense of security in our ability to dictate the direction of our lives. We erroneously feel like we're holding the wheel when, in reality, we may control our actions but God controls our outcomes.

The lesson here is that we aren't meant to try to understand our next steps. We are, instead, called to be like Christ. I've thought a lot about what this might mean—to "be like Christ." Although Jesus is God, co-equal with the Father, he was submissive to the will of the Father. Have you ever wondered about some of the things Jesus might have wanted in his state of humanity but knew he wasn't meant to have? I think there's an innocent element of human nature that allows us to desire something without the sin of coveting it. There are a lot of things we are permitted to dream about as long as we are committed to the ultimate plan of God. Is it so far-fetched to think of Jesus in this way?

We'll never know for sure, but I think it's fair to reason that Jesus may have wondered what it would have been like to have a wife and family, that he may have been intrigued by another profession outside of carpentry, that he might have longed for a lengthier life filled with comfort and peace as opposed to being brutally and unfairly murdered at the young age of 33. If given the chance, I'm sure he would have dodged the stinging pain from the loss of his earthly father, Joseph, and the ultimate betrayal from one of his best friends, Judas. And let's not forget his angst about facing the unfathomable agony of the cross itself. So much of Jesus' time here on earth isn't what any of us would elect to endure by choice, but the Lord had bigger things in mind and Christ was committed to his part in the plan.

Jesus' life was less than ideal from our human perspective. It was total perfection, however, in the eyes of God. Jesus was as much human as he was divine—that's what makes him the only one qualified to save us. He understands the longings of our hearts. He walked this earth, too, and he relates perfectly to our third-rock-from-the-sun vantage point. I think we forget this sometimes. I know I do. He asked for the Father to take the fate of the cross from him if there could be any other way, but the crucifixion was the only key to unlock heaven's gates for the rest of us. Jesus' heart followed the desires of his Father and he gave up his life of his own accord because he trusted that God was in control.

As Christians, we are forever grateful that he conquered the grave, but let's not lose sight of the reality that he felt genuine fear, pain, and devastating loneliness. He experienced human emotion no differently than you and I do today. That's mind-blowing to me and also something that motivates me to commit to my part of God's plan.

I know we'll never be in the divine shoes of our Savior, but I think it's important to relate to Jesus' humanity. He could love, hurt, breathe, and bleed just like us, and yet, in his perfection, he gave his earthly desires over to the bigger picture of God's purpose. Sometimes we long for "this" or "that" in the worst way, but it just doesn't work out for reasons beyond our understanding. Sometimes an opportunity arises that seems to be everything we've dreamed of only to find out it wasn't destined to be in our long-term scope.

How do we make sense of these scenarios? How do we know whether to choose door number one, two, or three? Which career route do we take? How do we come to terms with a tragic loss or a debilitating illness? How do we find meaning in the dark storm cloud that seems to constantly hover over our heads?

Wise judgment and correct perspective won't happen through an earthly point of view, and this is where I tend to fail time and time again. In fact, trying to focus our eyes horizontally as opposed to vertically will only cause us to be met with confusion, frustration, and an overwhelming sense of doubt as we keep trying to navigate our own paths. This life isn't about us. We exist to bring glory to our King, period. The sooner we embrace that, the sooner we will experience more meaning in each moment and greater peace in every situation.

So instead of pushing back, let's use the Word of God as our compass. Our road map for this life is found in the Bible. Specific scenarios may not be covered in full detail, but the basic principles of how we should live are spelled out in black, white, and red. I counseled with one of our pastors during the height of my medical mystery, and he gave me some of the most helpful advice I'd received in all of my searching. He told me that not every decision can be made based on the concrete foundation of "right" or "wrong." Instead, we should measure our choices based on what is "wise" and "unwise." The mileage I've gotten out of that has been invaluable.

So, devour your Bible, read devotionals and books that encourage a biblical mindset, surround yourself with people who will urge you to choose God and who will stand by you in the scary moments of uncertainty, and pray without ceasing. The more you submerse yourself in the things of God, the clearer God's wisdom will become.

Does this mean life will be easy, carefree, and overflowing with sunshine and rainbows? Truly, it might be the exact opposite. Jesus didn't walk an effortless path at all, but we know that he walked it well and accomplished far more than we can ever imagine because of his obedience. His earthly journey was one in which he would achieve his highest calling and bring the utmost amount of glory to his Father. No better joy can come from this life than to hear "Well done" from the lips of our God when we take our first step onto those golden streets.

My fellow navigators, please know that this life is not all that we are meant to experience. Some of us may not struggle much at all, some of us may encounter terrible suffering, and none of it may make any sense along the way. In the end, what will matter the most is how well we trusted in the One who lovingly paved our path. The fullness of our reward isn't found down here. Our treasures are laid up for us in heaven, so that's where our focus ought to lay.

Use God's Word as your matrix for evaluation and base your decisions on what is wise. Our Lord will work out the rest because his will is based on displaying his glory while showcasing his love, mercy, forgiveness, and hope. Take comfort in knowing that. Even if you feel as though you've made a thousand missteps, it's never too late to start utilizing the gift of wisdom. Begin now, pray for a heart that matches the Lord's, and move forward in the light of our eternal promise. Your time on earth will be filled with a reason for every circumstance, and heaven will hold your greatest reward!

I thought it appropriate to end this chapter with the chorus to one of my favorite songs that always fills my heart with encouragement, even in the bleakest of times:

When You don't move the mountains I'm needing you to move
When You don't part the waters I wish I could walk through
When You don't give the answers as I cry out to You
I will trust, I will trust, I will trust in You![1]

Insights

Have you ever taken the time to really think about Jesus as a human with real pain, real emotions, and real dreams? How does that help you better relate to him?

_____

_____

_____

_____

_____

_____

_____

---

1   Lauren Daigle, Michael Farren, and Paul Marbury, "Trust in You," *How Can it Be*, 2015.

What is it about life's darkness that bothers you most? Is it the unknown outcomes, the lack of control, the anticipation of lasting pain, or something else?

_____
_____
_____
_____
_____
_____

Actions

Have an honest conversation with Jesus. Pour out your fears and concerns for the things beyond the reach of your control. Ask him for strength and wisdom as you walk this path and thank him for being by your side, so you don't have to take these tough steps alone. Visualize him standing next to you when things get especially scary and lean on him for strength. His life wasn't easy, and his pain wasn't metaphorical. He really felt the blows of human life and he really comprehends whatever you're wrestling with on every level.

_____
_____
_____
_____
_____
_____

Chapter 13

Eternal ID

ENERGY ACCOUNT	
DEPOSIT	**WITHDRAWAL**
Identity Grounded in Christ	*Identity Grounded in the World*

This topic is the toughest one for me to tackle outside of the privacy of my own heart because I can't tell you with any level of confidence that I've even come close to conquering it. I'll be the first one to tell you that the exact opposite is true, and I struggle with letting go of any value that I feel may be accompanied by life's achievements. It's easy to see the worth in others, regardless of their vocation, connections, or successes. For me, however, it is a prideful sticking point that I've wrestled with my entire life.

When I first found myself out of work and staying at home after my medical issues progressed, I thought, "Maybe this won't be so bad! I'll have more time with my kids, I'll be able to pay more attention to my relationship with Brent, and I'll have less stress in my life and more time to work on improving my health." All of these things were true and were sincere blessings as a byproduct of my situation. I should have felt relieved and thankful to have been given the generous gift of time at this point in my life and there were moments when I bowed my head in gratitude.

But then some unknowing person would ask, "So what do you do for a living?"

"Uh," I'd reply, and then I'd word vomit all over them. "I sort of stay home at the moment due to a medical condition, but I used to be pretty talented in sales and account management. I was the primary breadwinner in my household. I did well for myself for several years."

Why? Why did I include my medical condition as some sort of justification for staying at home? Why did I feel the need to inject each line item of my resume as if this somehow made me more important as a person? What was so wrong with staying at home with three small kids who hadn't seen their mama with any scrap of consistency in, well, pretty much their entire lives? What was it about my former "achievements" that made me feel so big and my current situation that made me feel so small? Was focusing on my health and my family somehow inferior to a career path I'd spent my whole professional life trying to master? By no means. It wasn't an indication of failure or weakness. Quite the opposite. It took strength to make the initial decision to step away, dedicate my efforts to figuring out what was going haywire in my brain, and do what was best for my body and my family. Then why is it so hard for me to see it that way?

I know that pride is a major player (that five-letter "p" word has a wicked death grip when it comes to my ego). It seemed somehow impressive to tout my accolades packaged so neatly inside one of my various fancy titles over the years. People tended to "ooh" and "aah" and, to be completely honest, it felt exciting and fun to get that reaction. But, truthfully, who cares? Was it worth risking my health for a byline on a business card? Was it worth missing all the "firsts" that my kids accomplished without me as I threw myself into project after project? I can say with total confidence that the price was way too high and yet I still struggle with the topic at times.

Michelle Obama depicted this with incredible precision when she spoke on this subject in her book, *Becoming*:

> *This may be the fundamental problem with caring a lot about what others think: It can put you on the established path—the*

my-isn't-that-impressive *path—and keep you there for a long time. Maybe it stops you from swerving, from ever considering a swerve, because what you risk losing in terms of other people's high regard can feel too costly.*[1]

Another layer of this was embedded in the fear of not feeling confident. I was comfortable in my career. I knew the drill, I played the game well, I had a natural ability to perform at a high level, and I loved all the warm fuzzies that came with all of it. Each pat on the back, each "atta girl," each positive performance review, and each pay raise set the tone for my justification of pushing myself beyond a healthy limit and depleting my energy account. It also came at the cost of missing out on priceless time with the beautiful family I had waiting for me at home.

The thought of starting over, leaving behind the things I knew to expect for staying home, and having to learn a "new normal" was terrifying. What if I was bad at it? What if I did my children more of a disservice by being the single most present person in their little lives (the women at the daycare were pretty darn amazing at caring for our kids)? Could I learn to get good at this stay-at-home mom position? These questions might seem a bit dramatic and ridiculous, but I had never known any other way. On top of that, removing the daycare folks from my little ones' lives on a daily basis and completely switching up each of their set routines made the whole ordeal even tougher. This impacted *all* of us.

The final factor that played into my insecurities was plain and simple—money. I had a healthy salary that made up two-thirds of our total income. It afforded us the ability to do just about anything we wanted. We took awesome vacations, bought the coolest Christmas gifts, threw birthday parties that were larger than some small weddings (I'm a bit embarrassed to admit that I'm not exaggerating). We had freedom, but that freedom came at a cost. My career was forged on the back of a 24/7 business that doesn't lend itself to a 9 to 5 schedule. There were intricate proposals that needed to be meticulously drafted, meetings that ran long, flights

---

1   Michelle Obama, *Becoming*, New York, Crown Publishing Group, 2018, 91.

that got delayed or canceled altogether, critical customer needs that popped up after hours.

I also had a hard time, personally, fighting the urge to check emails or take phone calls once I was supposed to unplug and give my family what was left of my tattered attention. Some of these scenarios were out of my control and some were simply playing on my Type A personality. Either way, I was working *way* more than I was present with the most important people in my life, and for that I take full blame.

When I had to go on disability, my income was cut in half overnight. You know what was pretty incredible? We survived! We eliminated all the fat, and we didn't fall apart. Money isn't everything, you guys. We've discussed it earlier in this book. Those Golden Handcuffs are real. Once they're removed, we are free from their grip, but if they've grown tight enough, their impression remains for a little while. It can often take time to move on from a more lavish lifestyle, but it's worth every lost cent.

Now, to be clear, being successful at a particular career outside of motherhood (or fatherhood) isn't wrong and making an honest healthy wage to support your family is not a sin. What is a sin, however, is finding your identity in your abilities, successes, and financial status rather than in the One who created you for more than these things could ever amount to on their own. Hoisting commendations, titles, and money to the top of your priority list is a blazing red flag indicating that you've got it all backward.

I have intentions of going back to some version of a career in time should I feel the Lord's calling to do so. God has given me strengths that lend themselves to serve him in a professional capacity, and I'm hopeful that he may institute a plan for me to jump back in responsibly whenever and wherever it makes sense. And while I desire to move forward one day, I also know that it is critical to learn from my previous mistakes. Throughout these past 15 years, I've been given choices to make and I have often failed to steady those choices in sound biblical truths. Instead of establishing boundaries and setting a reasonable pace, I chose to exhaust my energy account by putting all of my worth in the characteristics of my career over replenishing my balance by resting in my existence as a child of God.

This particular war is far from over for me. I fight it daily. If I feel myself slipping back into my old habits, I pray for the strength to step away and request others to hold me accountable as well. I'm also working toward not resenting my current position in life. Instead, I'm experiencing the joy of being home with an 8-year-old who is watching my every move and growing into a little woman before my eyes; a 4-year-old goofball who is a mama's boy with every fiber of his being; and an almost 2-year-old who is a taking me on the irreplaceable journey of witnessing all of her precious firsts.

I am learning to cook healthy meals for my family, and I have the time to just sit and drink a cup of coffee with my husband as we talk about nothing in particular. I can go to my parents' house and enjoy lunch with them as I hear stories I hadn't been privileged to know in my past rushed existence. I'm cherishing phone calls with friends and finding opportunities to bless those in need. I finally have time to write with intentionality as I journal, blog, and, well, compose a book! There are so many more things on this beautiful list.

So, what's my title now? Child of God and Follower of Christ! Everything beyond that will fall into place organically as I keep trusting in the stillness of the Lord. My identity is rooted in him and him alone.

Therefore, as you received Christ Jesus the Lord,
so walk in him, rooted and built up in him and established in the faith,
just as you were taught, abounding in thanksgiving.
~COLOSSIANS 2:6–7~

Insights

Being completely honest with yourself, where do you find your identity truly lies? Is it grounded heavily in the fact that you're a child of God or do you place your worth in your job, your friends, your income, your appearance, your parental status, etc.?

_____

_____

Now that you've identified some of the areas you've formed your identity in outside of Christ, how do you think you would respond if one or more of these identity platforms were suddenly pulled out from underneath you?

_____
_____
_____
_____
_____

Actions

List anything you feel distracts you from the reign of Christ on the throne of your heart.

_____
_____
_____
_____
_____

Pray through the list you've made. Ask God to help you to minimize the priority of each "identity thief" and to elevate the Lord himself to the top of your list.

_____
_____
_____
_____
_____

Chapter 14

Take a Breath and a Step

ENERGY ACCOUNT	
DEPOSIT	**WITHDRAWAL**
Breathing in Life as It Comes	*Fighting God Every Step of the Way*

There is complete irony in the name of this chapter as it relates to the physical state I'm in while writing it. It's borderline comical actually. I'm on crutches right now from a knee surgery I had a week ago. This chapter is entitled "Take a Breath and a Step" and yet I feel like I can't breathe from the frustrations mounting around my current "new normal." And taking a step, well, that's certainly out of the question for a while.

Here's the story. I went in for what was supposed to be a simple meniscus repair. The recovery time was going to be quick and my knee problems were supposed to disappear into my rearview mirror. *Finally*, something fairly simple, straightforward, and completely fixable. Maybe, just maybe, this little corner of my chaotic world would be easy breezy and left in the dust of days gone by.

Nope, no dice. I woke up from my procedure to a weird look on the surgeon's face. "What?" I mumbled, knowing there had to be some not-so-great news looming behind her this-didn't-go-as-expected expression. She explained to me that what appeared to be a torn meniscus on the MRI was actually a piece of cartilage that had floated in front of the image. Once she got in and took a peek for herself, my meniscus was perfect. My cartilage, on the other hand, was shredded, and two pieces were actually completely broken off. She had to clean up that hot mess and then proceeded to perform what's called a microfracture procedure which involves drilling into my bone to encourage the marrow to come out and hopefully produce new, healthy tissue (my apologies to those of you with queasy stomachs).

So now here I sit, still trying to let it sink in that my recovery time is roughly triple what it was supposed to be, and I'll need a total knee replacement at some point as this is rarely a permanent fix. As my focus shifts inward, my thoughts begin to spiral, "I'm already in pain all the time, and now *this*? Lord, seriously, can I catch any sort of break? How is this even fair?"

But then I pray, I cry, and I pray some more. "I trust you, Lord. You've got some purpose for this. I know you've called me to be still. Clearly, you're using this time to reinforce what you feel I haven't quite mastered yet." Over this past week, I've been given the gift of help—help I hate to ask for but can't function without right now. Our families and friends have graciously stepped in so I can heal, and this has given me precious and rare time to write and reflect—time I probably would not have had otherwise. They've given me time to ponder the fact that I'm still not finding peace in circumstances outside of my control, time to continue to grow in the area of allowing others to assist, time to pray about and reconcile God's calling on my life and my future, and time to think about time itself—how precious it is and how little of it we are granted when we consider it relative to eternity.

So, as I stand, figuratively, in the presence of my Maker, I'm relishing this opportunity to soak up the Son. This entire journey has been remarkable, to say the least. Never could I have predicted *any* of this—and it seems the surprises just keep coming—but I'm slowly learning to accept them with a confidence in Christ that is stronger than it was before. None of this was an accident; nothing that has happened to me and my family fell anywhere outside of the will of God. He has purposed every providential detail and I've emerged forever changed and infinitely more grateful.

You know what else is ironic? I wouldn't alter any of this. Not a twist, a bump, a bruise, or a bum knee. These scars were formed through some of my darkest moments, but they are distinct marks forged from my personal battles. Each one is caught in the unfaltering grasp of my Creator's steady grip—his character, persistent devotion, and unfailing love. He never once let me fall outside of his reach. Each ding tells its own tale about where I was, how far I've come, and how much hope I have in where I'm headed. I may not have a pulse on the details, but I know how the story ends. It will end with a slowly sanctified version of me glorifying God in whatever way he sees fit as he refines me in the flames of this life.

There will undoubtedly be more mess-ups and wrong turns on my behalf. Imperfection is still woven into my flawed nature, but the Holy Spirit will persist in guiding me, nonetheless. So, with that, I'll take a breath and a step and continue forward in whatever direction God has for me. I encourage you to do the same, friends. Hope is on the horizon; you just need to breathe deep and step out in faith.

Insights

What unexpected curveballs have come your way and how have you handled them?

_____

_____

_____

_____

_____

How you have felt the presence of God as you endured the chaos?

_____

_____

_____

_____

Actions

Look back at some of your past trials (you might even be going through a tough one right now). List out all the ways that you've been molded, changed, stretched, and grown as a result of these hardships. Take some time to thank God for strengthening your faith in the fire.

_____

_____

_____

_____

_____

Chapter 15

Dear 43-Year-Old Me

ENERGY ACCOUNT	
DEPOSIT	**WITHDRAWAL**
Letting Your Past Guide You into Your Future	*Being Held Back by Hang-Ups and Habits*

Dear 43-Year-Old Me,

It has taken me a long time to work up the nerve to compose this final chapter, to write down all of the thoughts and dreams I have for you when you reach this age. It's been a bit excruciating actually. The details swirl around in my head like fireflies on a beautiful summer night. They're bright, illuminating, and oh-so enticing, but they also come with a fear of something quick to burn out or hard to catch. Chasing your passion is not for the faint of heart, and there are so many ways these next few years can play out. But that's not for you to agonize over. Your job is solely to learn from this journey, trust in God's plan for your future, and put one foot in front of the other as you continue to step out in faith. *Take a breath and a step,* remember?

So, as I think of all of the specifics and wonder through all of the "what-ifs," I've decided that none of these things are really for me to speculate about, nor are they things I think would be wise to spend my energy on. Instead, my desire is to prioritize what I want most for your heart, soul, and mind.

It's not notability for being an overachiever—you've been there, done that, and realized how quickly that can get out of control.

It's not a hefty income that pays for every earthly want you can possibly conjure up. You've already experienced the luxury of commanding a strong salary and yet happiness didn't result from those impressive paychecks.

It's not even necessarily for your illness to be completely cured. While one part of me hopes for total healing, another side of me has had a front-row seat to the lowest version of yourself as you painfully sifted through the smoldering ashes of who you once were. You've managed to slowly begin to conquer these physical demons that, at one point, crushed your entire being. You are so much better for these guardrails in your life now, for this new innate desire to never go back to the way things used to be. Your energy account has finally found some semblance of balance—a state of give and take that can allow you to flourish as a result of these beautiful lessons learned. Never in your life have you been so centered, and it's an amazing feeling that I pray continues until you enter into eternity.

Now that you've reached 43 (Lord willing), I hope your happiness stems from a place of humility and that you are living out your passion for others in some meaningful, Christ-focused way. I hope that you are less concerned about the thoughts of those impressed by what you do and more concerned about the thoughts of the one you serve. You are enough under the wings of his grace. You need to know this. I pray that you are more kind, more generous, more loving, and more patient than you have ever been because so many of those who had a part in your story had to be those things for you to pull you through your darkest hours.

I hope you find peace. Not just any peace, but that deep, Holy Spirit-indwelling peace that passes all human understanding. I hope you are unshakable in tough times—a kingdom force to be reckoned with—and that you are a beacon of light and hope for whoever comes after you with their own crosses to bear. I plead with you to share your story and share it often. Don't hold back, but instead be bold. Use your stormy voyage as a blessing that will have ripple effects like a stone skipped across the glassy water of time and experience.

I hope you are brave and learn to let go. I beg you to keep working on getting out of your own head. Your strength comes from the Lord; you are never responsible to conjure up this level of power on your own nor are you entitled to take the glory for anything good that comes from it. Stand your ground, know your place in this life, and honor your heavenly Father in the process. The rest of the abstract pieces of this crazy puzzle aren't always yours to put together and you have to be okay with that. Stop trying to be the god of your own universe. You're not qualified for that position. Leave it to the one who created you and who knows you more deeply than you'll ever know yourself. He's got you, he loves you, and he only has your best in mind.

Finally, please take the time to enjoy your life. This is one of those simple pleasures God intends for all of us to embrace. Stop missing the little things because you're too busy checking so many items off of your impossible, mile-long to-do list. Most of it will get done in time and the rest of it was never really that important anyway. The Lord, your husband, your kids, your family, and your friends—*they* are the ones who should be front and center on your playing field, not waiting for you on the sidelines. Cherish them, never take them for granted.

Nothing is promised and each moment is precious. Play, laugh, hug, jump in the deep end, let loose, and be a little goofy. Your heart will thank you and you might even learn how to truly relax. This is a gift you've never quite allowed yourself to receive. Take it with open arms and never view it as laziness or let it become mundane. It will fill your life with more joy than you ever thought possible and you'll be able to look back without regret.

I want you to know that I'm already proud of you. I'm proud of how far you've come and the legacy you are working so hard to leave behind. You still have so much to figure out, but you've learned to rise above your fears and face your challenges head on. Never forget that you dove into the depths of your soul and emerged a completely changed person. You've been rattled and shaken to the very core of your being and came out of it forever altered and wired for using these God-given lessons to inspire the goodness in yourself and those around you. You have nothing to prove, nothing to reach for, nothing to compete for outside of living a life that's pleasing to the Lord. He'll take it from there. But you already know this. I know you and I know you'll use these next few years to accelerate your growth in an even more positive direction. I'm beyond excited to see what the future holds as you walk this unmarked path. To God be the glory forever. Amen!

I can't wait to meet you,
38-Year-Old Me

Insights

What are some topics that struck a chord with you as you worked your way through this book?

In what ways have you begun to invest in your energy account? What are some additional things you hope to implement as you continue to grow?

Actions

Write a letter to your future self (pick any age that's meaningful to you). Include your lessons learned, your hopes and dreams, and all the ways in which you intend to hand the purpose of your life over to the will of Christ. Make it a habit of reading this letter from time to time to remind yourself of your desire to live out the rest of your days as a follower of Jesus and a force for his kingdom!

_____

_____

_____

_____

_____

_____

_____

_____

_____

_____

_____

_____

_____

_____

_____

_____

_____

_____

_____

_____

Acknowledgments

First and foremost, thank you to my Lord and Savior for turning my tragedy into triumph, for creating a masterpiece out of mayhem, and for providing calm amid the chaos. Your love, perseverance, and presence in my life go beyond my human comprehension and I'm forever grateful for your grace, forgiveness, and allowance of new beginnings.

To Cherry Lyn Hoffner, my editor and friend, where do I even begin? You've ridden this roller coaster with me through to the end. Thank you for your expertise and also for your kindness, your accountability, and your genuine heart. I couldn't have done this without you!

To Tim Beals and his top-notch team at Credo House Publishers, thank you for guiding this "new girl" through the publishing process, demonstrating such patience and professionalism as we navigated each piece together, and for believing in my project. You've made my dream a tangible reality!

Last, but never, ever least, a great big, huge, ginormous *thank you* to Brent, my kiddos, my family, and my friends. Not only have you watched me walk the challenging road of writing a book, but you've also lived every moment of this book with me. You've stuck by my side in my darkest moments, prayed me through my toughest times, and held me up when I didn't have the strength to stand on my own. You are my tribe in every sense of the word! I love you guys!

Hi, I'm Kelley

Kelley Wotherspoon is a Christian, wife, mother of three, author, business development professional, and domestic violence survivor advocate. She is always refining the art of balancing the elements of living, working, laughing, and serving.

A lifelong writer to the core, Kelley has also authored a children's book entitled *When I was a Baby* (available on Amazon.com or on WotherspoonBooks.com) created to help her oldest daughter understand that a parent's love grows, as opposed to divides, when another baby comes on the scene.

Kelley is passionate about using her life experiences to help you find joy in the hard stuff and to encourage your spirit. For reflections on how raising three kiddos with her husband while navigating chronic, neurological deficits can relate to your own struggles, read her *HINDSIGHT'S 30/40* blog on *WotherspoonBooks. com*. Follow her on social media via Facebook (*@Wotherspoon Books*), Instagram (*@wotherspoon_books*), and LinkedIn (*@Kelley Wotherspoon, MBA*) to catch her latest blog posts, stay in the loop on upcoming works, and follow her heart right on your screen with her video blog, *Coffee & Christ: Perk Up Your Soul.*